**IT'S NOT YOUR EMERGENCY:
THE GUIDE TO 911 DISPATCH**

I wasn't always an emergency dispatcher. By the time I entered the industry, I had already spent a decade as a professional musician and several more years as a small business consultant and a martial arts instructor. Unlike most of the wet-behind-the-ears kids in my dispatch class, I already had a few gray hairs before I took my first 911 call.

I've always made it a point to help people. When I opened my recording studio, my goal was to help local artists get their music out into the world. Later, when I started working with small business owners, my goal was to help people realize their dreams. Unfortunately, I had to learn, over and over again, that people will often do their best to take advantage of your kindness. I lost a lot of time and money this way. I figured that getting into emergency medicine would be a good way to help others without having to rely directly on those I was helping in order to pay my bills. Plus, I'm always looking to learn something new and there is *a lot* to learn about medicine. Initially, I wanted to get into emergency rescue – high angle, swift water and the like. I still do. At the time I was looking to make the transition, a friend recommended that I apply to the dispatch job that was open at the agency she worked for. I figured it would be a good foot in the door for a future career as a rescue paramedic. Once I began dispatching, I realized it was more interesting than I had expected. Plus, when it's 110° outside, I get to sit in an air-conditioned room.

During my time as a musician, I played for several notable artists and I always enjoyed being in the background instead of the spotlight. Being in dispatch is a lot like that. You get to play an important supporting role, while not being in the spotlight. Your efforts will certainly go unappreciated, but if your goal is to help others, then recognition shouldn't be a concern.

When I got hired for dispatch and was getting ready to start the training program, I thought I would get as many resources as possible so I could be extra prepared for class. While it was easy to find information about emergency medicine, I couldn't find any valuable resources for emergency dispatch. There were a few videos online of dispatchers talking about their job – but I wanted to know what to *really* expect. Not only the day-to-day of the job, but what I would need to know to be great at my job. Over the course of my training and in the next many months thereafter, I set about trying to become the expert in all things dispatch.

This book started as a short training manual for those who would be training at my own agency. As a dispatch preceptor, I train new employees once they have completed their classroom training and are ready to get out on the floor. Through this training process, I discovered a number of skills that could be gained before and during the training process. As I started writing, I realized that the gap in information available to new dispatchers around the world needed to be filled. As I kept writing, my little training manual grew exponentially and turned into a book. My goal is to give you enough knowledge to know what you're getting into, to help you make it successfully through the hiring and training process and to give you tools to excel on your own as a dispatcher. The majority of the examples I've used are in relation to EMS or fire dispatching, as that is what I specialize in. However, you should find most of these lessons to be universal no matter what field of dispatch you choose to go into.

    I've organized this book into four main sections. The first section is designed to help you get a job as a dispatcher, to pass the testing, interview and training process. If you're already an emergency dispatcher, you can probably skip over this section. Though, you might want to share it with any friends or family interested in entering the industry.

    In the second section, I discuss some of the skills that can be helpful to you as a dispatcher. Every call is different and our ability to adapt and problem solve are invaluable to getting care to our callers. Many of these skills come with time and trial and error. I've decided to share some of my tips and tricks so my errors can be your lessons.

    Section three is about the arts of Aiki and Zen in the dispatch environment. Through my years of studying eastern philosophy and martial arts, I've learned some skills to help keep both my patients and myself calm. These stories and ideas were selected to be helpful to all dispatchers, new and old.

The final section is a collection of stories from the dispatch chair. Most of them are calls that I've taken personally. Some have been contributed by my colleagues. Some are funny, some are sad – all are representative of what you can expect when you put on your headset for the first time.

If you have any questions about dispatch, would like to discuss Aiki or Zen or have any stories to share for the next edition of this book, please feel free to email me at tweedjefferson@gmail.com.

Tattoo inside your eyelids this reminder:
'You are the messenger, not the message. You are just like everyone else.' This was the advice given by a charismatic Zen teacher to a class of Zen teachers-in-training.
"What do you mean?" they asked her.
"I'll begin with a story about a besieged town that was surrounded by enemies who would slaughter all the inhabitants if help didn't arrive. Just when things looked hopeless, a messenger slipped through enemy lines with the message that the army of the Shogun would attack in the morning and drive off the invaders.
"The townspeople were so enraptured with this news that they treated the messenger like a hero. And after the Shogun's army left, they elected the messenger mayor. Though a pleasant fellow, the messenger turned out to be a thoroughly inept leader and was soon sent away in disgrace.

"The lesson here is never confuse the message with the messenger. You are only a messenger.
"When you stun an audience with the wisdom of a lecture, when your students cede to you the molding of their minds, when you are treated as someone special, focus on the message inside your eyelids:
You are the messenger, not the message.
You are just like everyone else."

SECTION I:
SO YOU THINK YOU CAN DISPATCH

BEFORE YOU PICK UP THE PHONE

When I was first recommended to the dispatch job by a paramedic friend, I thought that I would maybe spend a couple of days shadowing another dispatcher and would be off to the races, taking exciting calls and saving lives on my own. Imagine my surprise when I attended orientation and learned that the hiring process and training program was over three months long. At least they would be paying me while I was training!

Training programs vary from agency to agency – your training program may, in fact, just be sitting in with another dispatcher for a few days before they turn you loose on your own. If you're looking to work for a larger agency, expect a more intensive training program. Due to county policies, IAED protocols and liability concerns, there likely will be a virtual bible of policies and procedures that you will need to learn. Hopefully, by sharing my own experiences, you'll have a better idea what to expect.

The whole process began for me with completing an application online, followed by a large group orientation, a dispatcher aptitude test and several interviews before being selected to attend the training program. Out of about eighty applicants who attended the orientation, only eight made it to the class. Only four of those made it from the class to the dispatch floor. What follows in this chapter is a basic explanation of the hiring and training process.

APPLICATION AND ORIENTATION

Your typical, modern agency will have job openings posted on their website along with a hiring portal where you can apply online. The job application itself is pretty standard – personal information, job history, certifications, references, etc. Unless this is the first job you've ever applied for, you're probably pretty familiar with the format. I will caution you to be completely honest and transparent on your application. Many departments include background checks as part of their hiring process. Several applicants with minor infractions in their past have been let go after starting the training process due to dishonesty on their application. However, several dispatchers who have been on the floor for many years have misdemeanors or felonies on their record but were honest about it from the start of the hiring process, so it was not held against them.

Those whose applications were selected were invited to attend orientation, a large group meeting in a classroom. The purpose of which is to let us all know what would be expected of us through the training process and once we were on the dispatch floor. To a lesser extent, it was to scare away those who wouldn't take it seriously enough from the rest of the process, to save time and money on training anyone who wouldn't cut it. Surprisingly, out of the forty-or-so applicants who attended my orientation, about 90% of them showed up in sweat pants, tank tops, pajamas, etc.

I know they said that the orientation was casual dress, but you're applying for a job here, it's not too much work to look even somewhat professional. Maybe they aren't judging you this early in the hiring process, but they probably are – and they should be. Bring a pen and a notebook, even if you don't think you'll need it.

CRITICALL TEST

The CritiCall test is the universal aptitude test for emergency dispatchers. Whether you plan on working in law enforcement, fire or EMS, you can expect to take this test. Some limited information on the test can be found online, but I was unable to find any kind of practice test or study guide. My hope, over the next several pages, is to give you a general explanation of each section of the test, as well as a few sample questions, so you can be more prepared to take the test. Each agency has the ability to add or remove sections of the test, so you may not see all of these on your test, but the general concepts should be fairly universal. I've also included a short paragraph after each test segment regarding *why* these skills are important in the dispatch environment.

A few notes about taking the test: The entirety of the test will be taken on a computer. When you are taking the test, there will be an explanation and set of sample questions for each section of the test. You may opt to do this sample section or to skip it. Since the time limit for the test is generally around two hours and each of these practice sections take five to ten minutes each, I recommend that you do not do the practice for each test section, as you may not have enough time to finish the test. Limit your practice segments to two or three sections – whichever you feel you may have the most difficulty with. The majority of test-takers use the entire two hours. Also, there is no set pass or fail score; this is determined by the hiring agency. They may opt to just take the top five candidates from a testing pool, or they may set their own minimum score. With my agency, the minimum score is eighty percent and they only take the top ten candidates from that pool. Less, if an insufficient number of candidates pass with the requisite score. You'll be wearing headphones throughout the test which will both provide you with instructions and give you audio data for particular sections of the test.

Typing Test: The first section of this test is pretty standard. On the top half of your screen, you'll have the original text, which you'll need to retype in the bottom half of the screen. I believe the standard "passing" score for this section is about 35 wpm. There's no need to try to race to the end. As far as I can tell, it's a timed test with no actual end, versus something you can get to the end of. I type in the 65 wpm range and I was nowhere near finishing the document when the timer ran out – if there even is an end. Accuracy counts, so be sure to get all spelling and punctuation correct. You won't get penalized for making a mistake, but you will get penalized for failing to correct your mistake. Do some practice tests online to prepare and don't worry about trying to beat the clock.

Selecting the Agency: Beginning after the typing test and throughout the entirety of the rest of the test, a bell will ding and in the bottom right-hand corner will be a box with a short explanation of a problem nature and four boxes: police, fire, medical and utility. For example, the box will say "Someone is robbing the convenience store" and you should click the button for police. Or, "My grandmother has passed out" and you should select the button for medical. Utility would be something like an electrical line down or a gas line rupture even though, in reality, we dispatch the fire department for these types of calls.

You'll be given four or five of these to practice with to get the feel of it – you have five seconds to complete each request. Once you've completed the first few examples, you'll move on to the next section of the test. However, throughout the rest of the test, about every sixty to ninety seconds, the bell will ding and you'll have to select the agency while still completing the other segment. I found this to be the most interesting and enjoyable section of the test. Though, it can be quite a challenge when trying to record more complicated information, such as a vehicle license plate and VIN.

The purpose of this exercise is to test your ability to multitask, your ability to resume what you were doing when a distraction occurs and your ability to make decisions quickly.

Entering Data from Text: The majority of the next several test sections have to do with data entry and attention to detail. Beginning with this first segment, the data-entry sections will become progressively more difficult. In this section of the test, various information will be provided in one window and you will need to fill in the appropriate blanks in the simulated CAD (computer aided dispatch) screen.

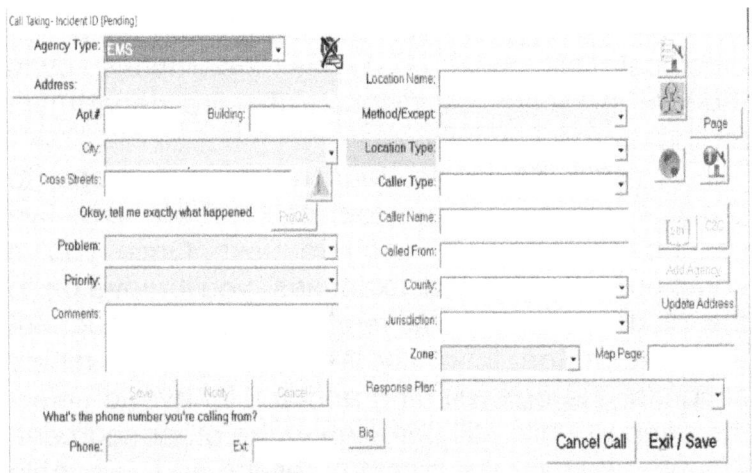

Sample CAD Screen

This is basic information like name, address, phone number. The information may or may not be presented in the same order as it will go into the

CAD, so you'll need to be able to quickly move between the fields using Tab and Shift-Tab or the mouse.

Entering Sequential Data from Audio: The next segment of the data-entry section of the test is similar to the first segment, except that instead of the data being presented in text, it will be read to you through headphones and in the order of the CAD screen. Thankfully, it's read clearly and slowly, so most people should have no problem hearing the letters and numbers as they are provided. The mock-caller typically reads the information as such: "My name is Mike Jones. M-I-K-E J-O-N-E-S. My address is 123 Colton Street. That's 1-2-3 C-O-L-T-O-N Street". You won't be allowed to write anything down for the duration of this test, so it will be up to you keep up as the data is presented, but compared to later sections of the test, this should be a breeze.

The cornerstone of 911 dispatching is collecting the information from the caller. You'll find yourself entering data into fields over a hundred times per day in a busy call center. Being able to do so quickly and accurately is one of the most important traits of a good dispatcher.

Entering Random Data from Audio: Essentially the exact same as the previous segment, except the data is randomized. If the fields listed are Name, Address, Phone Number, License Plate

Number, Comments, for example, in the previous section, the simulated caller would have provided you with all of the data in order, spelled out for you. In this section, they will present the data in random order, sometimes not spelling out or repeating the information.

Although we would like to collect information from callers in an organized fashion, the callers will often tell us a bunch of random information that doesn't fit with our carefully designed CAD screen. When this is the case, it's up to us to get the information input as we receive it. Asking callers to repeat information wastes valuable time and often frustrates callers.

Cross-Referencing Data: Continuing with the data-entry section of the test, you'll be given a list of a few dozen names, addresses and phone numbers. You'll be asked, for example, "What is the phone number of the person who lives at 342 Main Street?" or "What is the address for Jim Smith?" You'll need to look through the list and find the corresponding data set. The lists are not sortable and are in no particular order, so it's up to you to quickly scan the list for the information you need to find. The answers must be verbatim, so be careful of typos when entering your responses.

We often have to go back and look through our calls for information. Sometimes we'll just have a patient name or an address, but we need to provide as much information as possible to our crews or partner agencies as quickly as possible.

Simulated Call-Taking: This is the final and most difficult segment of the data-entry section of the test. If there were one section of the test that I would recommend taking the time to do the practice questions, this would be it. You'll listen to a simulated 911 call (thankfully, the caller is calm and not yelling at you). They'll give you any amount of information in any order and you'll type it into the designated fields or into a comments box. This could be anything from the standard name, address, phone number to vehicle license plate and VIN as well as their explanation as to why they are calling. Once the call has ended, you'll go to a screen that has five questions about the call. For example, the caller may state, "My name is John Doe, I live at 927 Willow Street. There's a suspicious blue car backed into my neighbor's driveway and they have been taking things out of the house and putting them into the trunk of the car. The license plate is 3VPN532. My neighbors address is 939 Willow and his name is Ted Johnson."

That's a lot of information to try to record as someone is speaking it, so you'll have to take what notes you can in whatever shorthand you're comfortable with. If you go into it thinking you only need to get the most pertinent information like address and license plate number, like I did, you'll

struggle with this segment. The questions about that previous section will be similar to:
- What is the address where this incident is taking place?
- Does the reporting party live on Willow Ave, Willow Drive or Willow Street?
- Which direction is the suspect vehicle facing?
- What items were taken out to the car?

So, as you can see, you'll need to be pretty diligent with your note taking and memory. And, like the fourth example question, there may even be some trick questions in there. And don't forget, the little box will continue popping up throughout, asking you to select the agency to dispatch a call to.

When taking calls, you'll often have to record little details that may be important later. In the community where I grew up there was a Revis Road, Revis Court, Revis Way and a Revis Circle all in a one-mile radius. You can see that having the right street name can be critical to getting someone the help they need.

Map Reading: If you're comfortable with your standard city map, this should be *very* easy for you. You'll be provided with simple three or four block map:

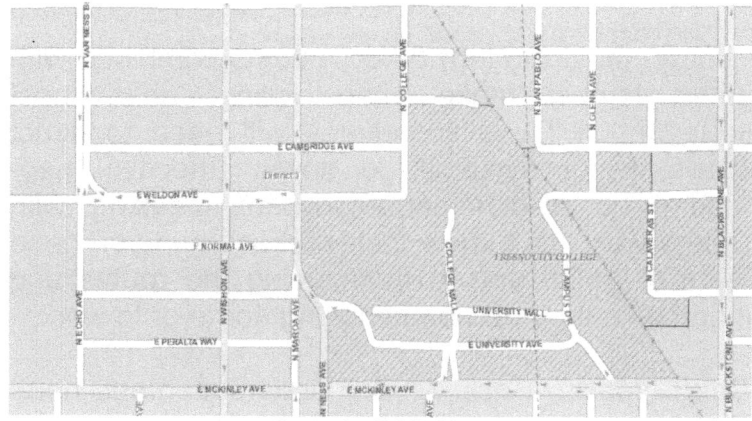
Sample CAD Map

The questions will be similar to:
- If you are traveling east on McKinley Ave and turn onto Wishon, which direction will you be heading?
- If you travel from Blackstone and McKinley, heading west, turn right on Van Ness and turn right at the next four-way intersection and go one block, which intersection will you be at?
- Which route would you tell an ambulance to take to get from College Mall and University Ave to Echo and Peralta?

Watch out for things like one-way streets and building entrances on the map, as they will intentionally give you questions that will entice you to overlook these sorts of things. For example, in question one, the arrows indicate that you can only turn right onto Wishon.

Though most modern CAD systems combined with smart-phones make map-reading an almost irrelevant skill, we sometimes will need to direct crews if our systems go down. Effective map-reading is also important when speaking with callers who don't know their address and you need them to guide you to them using the routes and landmarks they use when driving home or to work.

Basic Math: Basic is an understatement here. These are simple, grade-school level arithmetic problems. Sample questions may include: "Jim had 15 rugs, now he has 7. How many rugs are missing?" and "If the dispatch center handles 50 calls per day and dispatcher A handles half of them, Dispatcher B handles 20 calls, how many calls does Dispatcher C take?"

There isn't much more I can say about the math section. If you completed any middle-school level math class, you should have no problems with this.

Mixed-Up Words and Numbers: This section of the test has mostly to do with your attention to detail. You'll be given a word or a series of numbers and asked to match them to the correct answer.

Examples:

Match "87427"
- 84727
- 87427
- 84277
- 87472

Match "Michael Salomon"
- Michael Soloman
- Micheal Salomon
- Michael Salomon
- Michael Solomon

Not too difficult, right? Just take your time and double check your answers.

On the dispatch floor, when typing in addresses or looking up information, you'll have to make sure that information is correct. We can't help somebody if we go to the wrong address. If you get a sudden bout of dyslexia, it can be a matter of life and death in this job.

Recalling Phone Numbers: You will be provided with a seven-digit phone number, either via audio or on your screen. You'll get a couple of seconds to remember it, then it will disappear, or in the case of audio, will go to dead air for about five seconds. Then you'll be asked to type the phone number in as you remember it. Remember, you can't write anything down, so it'll be up to you to repeat the number over and over in your head, or think up a mnemonic device to help you remember the number.

We ask every single caller for their phone number in case we can't find them or need to call them back for additional details. Sometimes callers will give you an address then launch into their explanation of what's going on without giving you time to make sure you got the address input. Getting the phone number and address right the first time is critical to being able to do our jobs.

Recalling Alpha-Numeric Data: This is the same as the previous section but instead of being given a phone number, you'll be given a six-to-ten digit alphanumeric pattern to remember, so it will be a little more difficult. The process it the same, you'll see or hear the item for a few seconds, be given about five seconds to remember it, then have to recall it. The character strings may be something like "32A7BV98" or "GG9T554". Slightly more difficult, but shouldn't give you any problems if you are prepared for it.

It can be confusing to take information like vehicle license numbers over the phone. By paying attention to letter and number order, you'll prevent mistakes and extra work by getting those numbers right the first time.

Word Usage: I was going to call this the spelling section of the test, but you won't so much be asked to spell words so much as you'll be asked to select the proper word for a given sentence. For example: "The calling party said the accident happened in front of _____ house." (Select: They're, Their, There). Or, "The car is parked _____ to the curb." (Select: Parallel, Paralel, Parralel). If you're not one to consider yourself an English major, take a few minutes to look up commonly misspelled words or commonly misused words and read through those. The majority of these questions have to do with the most commonly misused words and spellings. Here are a few additional examples that I would recommend being familiar with both spelling and definition: waver/waiver, except/accept, effect/affect, loose/lose, bear/bare, two/too/to, week/weak, weather/whether.

The majority of dispatch centers enter comments into the CAD card that will be read by the crews. Proper word usage and spelling is paramount to making sure your crews have clear information when responding to a call.

Reading Comprehension: If you went to public school and took the annual assessment tests, you'll be quite familiar with this section of the CritiCall. You'll be given a couple of paragraphs to read and then be asked several questions about what you just read. For example:

"When another old cave is discovered in the south of France, it is not usually news. Rather, it is an ordinary event. Such discoveries are so frequent these days that hardly anybody pays heed to them. However, when the Lascaux cave complex was discovered in 1940, the world was amazed. Painted directly on its walls were hundreds of scenes showing how people lived thousands of years ago. The scenes show people hunting animals, such as bison or wild cats. Other images depict birds and, most noticeably, horses, which appear in more than 300 wall images, by far outnumbering all other animals. Early artists drawing these animals accomplished a monumental and difficult task. They did not limit themselves to the easily accessible walls but carried their painting materials to spaces that required climbing steep walls or crawling into narrow passages in the Lascaux complex. Unfortunately, the paintings have been exposed to the destructive action of water and temperature changes, which easily wear the images away. Because the Lascaux caves have many entrances, air movement has also damaged the images inside. Although they are not out in the open air, where natural light would have destroyed them long ago, many of the images have deteriorated and are barely recognizable. To prevent further damage, the site was closed to tourists in 1963, 23 years after it was discovered."

Which title best summarizes the main idea of the passage?
1. Wild Animals in Art
2. Hidden Prehistoric Paintings
3. Exploring Caves Respectfully
4. Determining the Age of French Caves

Based on the passage, what is probably true about the south of France?
1. It is home to rare animals.
2. It has a large number of caves.
3. It is known for horse-racing events.
4. It has attracted many famous artists.

According to the passage, which animals appear most often on the cave walls?
1. Birds
2. Bison
3. Horses
4. Wild cats

Why was painting inside the Lascaux complex a difficult task?
1. It was completely dark inside.
2. The caves were full of wild animals.
3. Painting materials were hard to find.
4. Many painting spaces were difficult to reach.

You won't be able to refer back to the story while answering the questions, so it's important to pay attention to detail. The stories aren't very long, so you may want to scan over them a couple of times to pick up any important information.

Callers will often give you long, convoluted explanations. It'll be up to you as a dispatcher to discern the most important information from their explanation and convey the most meaningful details to your crews.

Matching Word Pairs: In this segment of the test, you'll be quizzed on your ability to remember pairs of information and recall them. You'll be given three or four pieces of information to remember, then be quizzed on them. A couple of examples:

Red Boat, Green Car, Black Truck

"What color was the car?"

Salty Taco, Spicy Burrito, Cheesy Hamburger, Greasy Potatoes

"Which item was spicy?"

When you're on the floor, you'll need to remember a lot of information that callers will give to you faster than you can type. Remembering key details will be critical to your ability to keep up with the call and avoid asking callers to repeat information.

Best Conveying a Message: In the final section of the test, you'll be given a short paragraph and asked to choose the corresponding answer that *best* conveys the message. There may be multiple answers that are technically correct, but they are looking for the one that most specifically relates the information in the sample. Example:

"The car is parked outside of the hardware store. The car is in the front aisle. The car is facing the building. It is a red car. The car has a flat tire"

Select:
- Outside of the hardware store, there is a red car, parallel to the entrance.
- Near the hardware store is a car with a flat tire.
- The red car with a flat tire is parked perpendicular to the hardware store in the first aisle.
- Look for a red car, go to the hardware store. It has a flat tire and is in front of the hardware store.

The correct answer, in this example, is the third answer. Again, there are many correct answers, but one will best convey the information given in the clearest language. As a dispatcher, you'll be expected to do this on a daily basis while inputting caller comments into the cards.

So that's the whole test. I know it seems like a lot, but the two hours go pretty fast. If you complete this test with the requisite score, you may be asked to complete the next phase of the hiring process. In my case, this was a series of interviews.

INTERVIEWS

Coming from a background in business management, I was a bit taken aback by the interview process. The first interview was a panel interview, followed by two one-on-one interviews with members of upper management.

I was familiar with the standard job interview questions: "What are your greatest strengths/weaknesses", "Where do you see yourself in five years", etc. Even the more esoteric Silicon Valley interview questions wouldn't phase me. The panel interview was nothing like that. I sat across a table with three members of middle management and HR and they took turns asking me questions from a laminated card and scoring my answers. Here are a few of the questions I can remember:

- Describe a time where you went above and beyond the call of duty.
- Explain a challenge you had to overcome and how you dealt with it.
- Tell us about a specific time you had to deal with conflict and how you handled it.

- Talk about an accomplishment you had at work and how you achieved it.

This went on for about twenty minutes. I found it to be very uncomfortable, bureaucratic and impersonal. Leaving the interview, I didn't feel like they got to know who I was as a person at all. Fortunately, I did well enough to make it through to the next phase of interviews, which was a lot more fun. If you are prepared for this panel type of interview, you'll do a lot better than just going in expecting to chat with someone casually.

The second phase of the interview was pretty interesting. I came into the room to meet the communications center manager. He handed me two decks of cards and asked me to sort them – one deck by suit and the other in numerical order. Meanwhile, he read aloud a fairy-tale type story. As all this was going on, random staff members came in and started talking to us. At the end of the story and the card sorting, he asked me several questions about the details of the story he just read. Of course, the purpose of this interview was to test my ability to multitask as well as not get distracted by other things happening around me.

The third and final interview was with the communications director for the agency. She did, in fact, ask me questions about myself and gave me some of those standard interview questions I was prepared for. However, she had a radio scanner going in the background the whole time to serve as a distraction. Every couple of personal questions she asked me, she would play me a 911 call recording from her phone and ask me to gather as much information as I could about the call, which she would then quiz me on. The phone was quiet and the scanner provided enough cross-chatter to make it very difficult.

After passing that interview, all that was left was a drug test and physical fitness test. What kind of physical fitness test is required of a dispatcher? It isn't much. You have to bend over, squeeze a grip meter and lift a ten-pound box. It's pretty easy and almost seems silly to have someone go do it, but I'm sure it's another one of those liability things. We have individuals in our dispatch center with physical disabilities and they are able to do their job just as well as anyone else, so if you have a disability, don't let that stop you from pursuing a career in emergency dispatch.

IAED TRAINING

The International Academy of Emergency Dispatchers sets the national and international standard for dispatchers of all three disciplines. Their training and procedures increase patient care and response time while decreasing liability for the thousands of agencies who follow their protocols. I think their system is great and would encourage all agencies to look into getting accredited and their dispatchers certified.

As an emergency dispatcher, if your agency is accredited by the IAED, you'll have to get certified before you go out on the dispatch floor. The class for each discipline is two or three days long. For medical and fire together, it's a week long course.

In the course they explain the problem natures, the primary protocols we will use to select the responses of the crews and how to interrogate the callers.

For example, if a caller says they have trouble breathing, you would select the "Breathing Problems" problem nature and their protocol would provide you with relevant questions about their problem. Whereas the problem natures of "Psychiatric Problem", "Traffic Accident" or "Structure Fire" will provide you completely different questions to ask the caller. Each protocol will also provide you with instructions to give the caller specific to each problem nature. You wouldn't tell a caller with chest pain not to put out a fire any more than you'd tell an individual with a gas leak to take aspirin. These protocols give you the appropriate instructions to give for every kind of problem nature. There are at least thirty problem natures for each discipline and it may seem like a lot to know, but they follow a logical process and nearly any situation you can think of fits into one problem nature or another.

In addition to following the protocols, you'll be taught how to give first aid and CPR instructions over the phone. In the training classes, everything is calm and follows a script, unlike in the real world. However, by learning these procedures, you're better prepared to give help to a caller when they are in distress.

If your agency is IAED accredited and you are getting certified, my advice to you is to become familiar with each problem nature and the associated rules. The academy is very strict about everything being read verbatim and the protocols being followed exactly. An accredited agency is required to have an ED-Q review a particular percentage of their calls for compliance. This means that somebody will be listening to your calls to make sure you are asking every question and providing the appropriate instructions to the caller.

IN-HOUSE TRAINING

Unlike IAED training, which is universal around the world for accredited agencies, in-house training will vary. Typically, the training program is designed by your agencies management. There's no way I can tell you exactly what kind of training you'll go through, so I'll just explain my training and hope that it will give you an idea of what to expect.

Including the week of IAED certification training, classroom training for my agency lasted six weeks. Each week covered a specific area of study and was punctuated by a test every Friday. We were required to get an 80% on each test and failure to pass any two tests resulted in dismissal from the program. I know many agencies don't have quite as strict of policies for trainees, but given the high attrition rate, I can understand why they do it – no need to spend a lot of time on individuals who aren't taking it seriously or who are holding back the progress of the class. What follows is a brief summary of the topics we learned:

- Call cancelation policies.
- Upgrade and downgrade policies.
- Taking calls from medical facilities.
- Helicopter dispatch procedures.
- Problem natures and priority of response.
- EMS unit numbers and posts. Which units respond to particular types of calls.
- Fire apparatus types. The difference between engines, trucks, brush rigs, etc.
- Fire apparatus numbers and corresponding stations.
- Basic life support – CPR and first aid training.
- County EMS agency policies.
- Scene security procedures.
- Dispatch center policies (dress code, attendance, et al).
- Scheduled patient transfers.
- How to navigate the CAD and map systems.
- Bariatric patient policies.
- Radio frequencies and which agencies use each channel and for which purpose.

- Major cross streets and addresses for the cities in which we dispatch.

As you can see, there is a lot to learn before you can even walk out onto the dispatch floor. Nothing terribly difficult, but the sheer quantity of data requires regular study. In my class, those of us who met on the weekends and evenings to study all passed the class. All of those who thought they could just come to class during the day and skip the studying did not pass the class.

On the last day of class, we took a final that covered all of the material for the entire program. The test required an 80% score and failure to meet that score resulted in dismissal from the program. Half of our class did not pass the final because, even though they had passed the minimum amount of weekly tests, they did not continue to study the material from previous weeks. It will be up to you to make the time in your personal life to keep up on the material.

ON THE FLOOR TRAINING

Those who pass the class are sent out to the dispatch floor to train with an experienced dispatcher. This training lasts anywhere between four and eight weeks, depending on how the dispatcher trainee is doing.

Coming out of the class with a 99% overall score, I expected to just get on the phones and be ready to go – I knew all the policies, I was comfortable with the CAD, I knew all of the problem natures inside and out. Boy was I surprised when I finally got on the phones! In class, everything is calm and the information is provided clearly. On the phones with the general public, it's completely different. Callers are panicking, they don't speak clearly, if they speak English at all, everything has to be handled with a sense of urgency as not to delay patient care. When I started training new employees one of my fellow dispatchers told me, "If you don't think you were this bad when you started, you were."

Standard procedure for our training is on day one the new dispatcher just listens in as the preceptor takes calls, asking questions between calls. On day two, the trainee will type into the CAD while the preceptor talks to the callers. Day three the trainee will talk to the callers while the preceptor types into the CAD. Since we work alternating three and four day weeks, this is usually the end of week one for the trainee.

Starting with the second week, the trainee is on their own on the phones and CAD, with the preceptor listening in and helping as necessary. If the trainee gets lost or stuck on a problem nature, the preceptor can help them figure it out. As the weeks go on, the goal is to help them less and less.

Once the trainee is beginning to take calls on their own, the preceptor should discuss each call with them after they hang up. The preceptor will be looking to address any deviation from policy, ask them why they selected a particular problem nature and give them tips on how to deal with difficult callers. It's frustrating to just about everybody to have somebody hovering over them and correcting everything they do. After they have a little bit of experience, the preceptor should try to only interject when they make and error that can compromise patient care or scene safety.

Every preceptor is different and each trainee has their own strengths and weaknesses. Your experience will be unique to you. I've noticed a few things that many trainees struggle with and I'll discuss them so you can be on the lookout for them when you are training.

The majority of trainees lack confidence, especially in the beginning. Often they are afraid of making a mistake or saying something that they feel might upset a caller (or, you know, kill someone). The time to make mistakes is while you are training; you have someone there to notice and help correct your mistakes. You'll need to make mistakes to learn how to get yourself out of trouble. If following the protocols, the callers very rarely get angry or upset at you. The majority of callers who escalate do so because the dispatcher freelances, isn't listening to them or isn't communicating with them. I take around four hundred calls per week and usually have an average of one irate caller each week – and they are generally already angry before I even answer the phone. More about those callers in a successive chapter.

Often, we have to multitask when taking calls. In addition to speaking to the caller and entering information into the CAD, we need to be notifying crews and communicating with other public safety answering points (PSAPs). Depending on if your dispatch center is vertical or horizontal, you may need to be communicating with the crews over the radio while you're still on a call, or notifying the radio operators. New dispatchers will get so focused on the call they are on that they forget all of the other things they need to be doing. Work on being quick on the mute switch to speak to your colleagues while on the phone. Use those colleagues as resources to update crews and PSAPs while you are speaking with the caller. A great dispatcher will listen to what's going on around them and help their partners out preemptively. I've found that as long as you communicate with your caller, they won't get angry or frustrated. When I need to update a radio operator, notify a PSAP or address scene security, I'll tell the caller, "Just one moment while I speak with the paramedics/fire department". This easily buys me fifteen or twenty seconds to handle what I need to do and get back to the call.

Balancing speed and precision is another difficult skill to master. Our goal is to have the call into the system within thirty seconds of picking up the phone. This means getting and verifying the address and figuring out why they are calling in the first few seconds of the call. We tell our trainees not to worry about being fast in their first several weeks; their goal should be to be exact with their addresses and problem natures. As the old adage goes, "slow is smooth, smooth is fast". Remember, you can't help somebody if you don't send the crews to the right place, so take the calls at a pace where you can verify that all the data you have is correct. As you take several hundred calls, you'll find yourself more able to move around the screens quickly, as well as able to remember more about what the caller says, so you don't have to re-ask questions later.

The final difficulty I wanted to address is having an appropriate attitude for each caller. Many dispatch trainees operate at either a one or a ten, with no middle ground. One dispatcher I trained started off incredibly timid, unable to control his callers, regularly being yelled at or hung up on. I gave him some pointers on how to deal with difficult callers – how to take control of the call and assert authority. He took this to heart and began to practice it…with every caller. I spent the next several weeks trying to get him to recognize when a caller is being cooperative and to speak to them appropriately and to only ramp up his demeanor *when the call warranted*. It's important to realize that the majority of callers do want our help, so dealing with them in a kind, compassionate way the first link in the chain of complete patient care.

SECTION II:
YOU *WILL* MAKE MISTAKES

*Good judgement comes from experience.
Experience comes from bad judgement.*

WORKING ON YOUR OWN

I'll keep this section of the book brief. The majority of the skills you'll need will be gained by doing the job. There are so many variables, I couldn't possibly explain them all. What's most important is being able to deal with those unusual circumstances as they come up, let nothing be unexpected.

It's easy to get complacent. If I take a hundred calls in a day, ninety-five to ninety-nine of them will be the same thing every day. Old people fall down, someone's stomach hurts, a traffic accident occurs, someone wants to commit suicide, the grass is on fire. The vast majority of the calls I take follow an almost identical course. Though, a few times per week something unusual will happen. Someone will jump off a building or get trapped in machinery, a baby will drown or a gas line will explode - those sorts of things. When these kinds of calls happen, it's important not to get flustered or confused and remember to handle them the same as every other call: calmly and professionally.

In this chapter, I'd like to talk about a few of the common challenges we run into and some of the techniques I've found for dealing with them.

DECISION MAKING

When training, you'll have somebody with you, checking for any mistakes and coaching you through each call. Once you're on your own, you'll need to make decisions quickly and on your own. Of course, you can always ask your supervisor or colleagues if you have questions, but our job requires us to make immediate decisions with limited information in order to provide our patients with the best care possible.

Knowing your protocols and priority symptoms will be invaluable in interpreting what the caller is telling you and being able to determine the level of care they need. A typical caller may tell you, "She's a diabetic, has CHF, she was in the hospital two weeks ago for a fall and they let her out last week and for the last couple of days she has been really sick, maybe she has the flu. She's been vomiting and has a fever and is short of breath and she's so weak she can barely stand up. Janet, can you stand up? No, she says she can't stand up. And she has a headache and did I tell you she was vomiting?" There's a lot of information in those few seconds – some of the problem natures that a call-taker might want to select from that statement are: diabetic problems, heart problems, falls, vomiting, sick person, headache or fever. However, in this circumstance, I would select breathing problems. For one, it's happening right now, whereas some of the potential problem natures (falls, diabetic issues and heart problems) are not happening now. Breathing problems is also the highest priority symptom of the problems the patient is having now. Each agency responds differently to each problem nature, but in the case of the agency I work for, breathing problems gets a lights-and-siren response, while vomiting or fever would get a non-lights-and-siren response.

It will also be up to you to make decisions regarding scene safety, which units to send to a call and when to send additional resources. Once you take a few thousands calls, you'll be a lot more comfortable making those decisions. You'll make mistakes – we all do – what's important is that you notice your mistakes and make changes to fix them as quickly as possible.

SCENE SECURITY

Not only are we responsible for getting help to our callers, we have to look out for the health and safety of our crews. We deal with psychiatric issues, assaults, stabbing, gunshot wounds, animal attacks and more on a daily basis. If we send our crews into these situations unaware, we could end up with three patients instead of one. While there's no way we can predict every situation the crews can get into, we can use our judgement to prevent any additional injuries.

If the situation is questionable, you can ask the caller, "Is the patient violent?" and "Do they have a weapon?" – or, in the case of a first-party caller, "Do you feel violent?", "Do you have a weapon?" Of course, they may not tell you the truth, but in my experience, they often do; even the psych cases.

Here's a short list of problem natures that present scene security issues – if anything is questionable, don't hesitate to hold your crews back and send law enforcement or an appropriate agency to secure the scene:
- Psychiatric problems – Is the patient violent, do they have a weapon? Many times, they are just calling for help and will not be aggressive with the crew. Use your judgement based on the demeanor of the caller and what you hear going on in the background of the call.
- Assaults – Where is the attacker? Were weapons involved?
- Stabbing/Gunshot Wounds – Since you know there are weapons involved, don't send your crews in unless you know for sure the scene is safe.
- Hemorrhage/Laceration – What caused the bleeding? Does it pose a threat to the crew?
- Hazmat/Gas Leaks – These scenes need to be secured by trained individuals, such as the fire department Hazmat team. Notify local utility companies as well.
- Electrocution – Crews need to be advised of any potential electrocution in case the patient is still charged or electrical hazards are present. You may need to notify utility companies to shut power off at the source.
- Animal Bites/Envenomation – If an animal (dog, snake, bird, elephant) bites a person, we need to be sure that the animal is not

around to bite the crews when they get there. Contact animal control if in question.
- Overdose – Patients who have taken an excessive amount of drugs or medications can be unpredictable. If the overdose was intentional, they may violently oppose being treated. Use caution when sending crews to these calls and co-respond law enforcement if unsure.

Though I didn't include it on the list, it's worth mentioning that diabetic patients and seizure patients can often be unpredictable. Generally, it's not because they are trying to be intentionally violent, but because their medical condition often causes confusion. Medics will generally be trained how to deal with these situations, but if the patient has a history of being violent with crews or family members, it may be best to send law enforcement as well.

When training a recent intern we received a call that went as such: a work crew is moving some furniture out of a house. When they leave, everything is fine. They return thirty minutes later and two people are dead. For me, red flags are going off everywhere. I asked my trainee what she was thinking about during the call and she said, "Starting CPR". I told her that when two people randomly die at the same time, there are other concerns – hazmat, carbon monoxide, violence. All situations that I don't want to send a crew into. It ended up being a low-rate fentanyl operation. Fortunately, the crews were okay.

Mostly, it's common sense. Would you want to put yourself in that situation? If not, then consider getting reinforcements for your crews before you send them out.

DUPLICATE CALLS

I read recently about an individual who was hit by a bus in San Francisco. They said that over forty people called 911 to report it. Although the callers don't know how dispatch centers work, this can be a nightmare for us. Your county's policies might be different, but our policy is that if someone calls for an ambulance, we send one unless we can 100% guarantee that they are the same patient that has already been called for.

This happens all the time: A customer at a big-box retail store passes out or has a seizure. The patient's family member calls 911. The lady at the end of the aisle calls 911. Another customer tells the staff, who also call 911. Someone walking by two aisles away hears the commotion and calls 911.

Now we potentially have three or four ambulances going for one patient. Not a good use of our resources. What we need to do is verify with each caller that they are calling about the same patient.

There are two primary pieces of information that are easiest to verify whether the patient is the same or not – their name and their problem nature. If all four callers report the patient is having seizures and her name is Karen, problem solved. However, in a public place, as in this example, the callers often won't know the patients name, nor what the problem is. The family member may say she's having a seizure, while the bystander says she collapsed and the employee doesn't know what's going on. In this case, we can't verify that there aren't additional patients.

Some ways we can narrow it down are by getting the patients approximate age, gender, clothing description and exact location. Now, if we have each caller reporting that it's a 40-50 year old female in the electronics department wearing a green sweater, we can comfortably cancel the additional responders.

When this happens to you (and it will), keep an eye on your map screen to see if another call already exists at the address you've been provided. If so, open the existing card and see how much of the information you can verify with your caller. If your partner is on the phone with the other caller, work together to corroborate the information and prevent the dispatch of several ambulances.

Fortunately, our fire department policies aren't so strict. If ten people call in and say the grass is on fire on Central Avenue, we don't sent ten engines; we're going to just take it as one call and add comments from each caller to help get the most specific information possible.

CALLER DOESN'T KNOW ADDRESS

As we've already discussed, if we don't know where to send the crews, we can't help out the caller. Sometimes the caller won't know their address, as is often the case with children or people traveling or in public places. They may have just moved or they could be a hiker out in the woods. There are countless reasons a person may not know exactly where they are.

If you're lucky, they're calling you from a landline or their cell phone pings exactly on their current location. Though, Murphy's Law dictates that if they don't know their address, they will be calling from a cell phone with a location that is pinging 1,000 meters off.

When this happens, there are several things you can ask to get a better location. If they are at a residence, the go-to is to ask them to find a piece of mail. Even junk mail is a viable option. You can also ask them to go outside and look at the mailbox/door/curb for numbers and, if need be, go look at the nearest street sign. This is more effective in urban areas than in rural areas, where street signs and address markers are few and far between. I've had to get someone to go knock on their neighbor's door and ask the address before. If you can get the crews to the neighbor's house, they'll make it to the patient.

Since cell phones essentially all have map features now, you can ask them to put you on speaker and use the map feature of their phone to show their current address – or even their GPS coordinates. If there are multiple people there, have them get a bystander to look up the address while you continue talking with the caller.

If none of those solutions work, you can ask the caller to give you street-by-street directions on how to get to their location. Follow along on your map and you can at least get the crews close enough to get waved down. If they can't do that, you can always ask them for the phone number of someone who does know the address or can give directions and have your partner call and get the information for you.

If you need to work from landmarks, that's another option. If they say they are by a school (and hopefully can give you a name), you can ask them if they are by the playground or by the parking lot. Your satellite map will be useful in working from landmarks.

Hopefully their cell phone will ping less than a hundred yards from their actual location. When this is the case, you can use street view to find them by business or street sign names. I had a caller downtown one night who didn't know where she was and she couldn't read, but she could spell the words. I had her start spelling the words from nearby signs. The first thing she spelled was, "P-A-R-K-I-N-G". Believe it or not, we still found her.

Public places are a lot easier. If you can get the business name, you can just use a search engine or your CAD presites to find the address and confirm you have the right location by providing the caller with the major cross streets. Or just have them give the phone to an employee, who usually knows the address or, at the very least, the intersection.

HYSTERICAL CALLERS

It doesn't happen as much as you might think, but on a fairly regular basis, you're going to have to deal with callers who are just out of control. They are either angry, panicking or both. They don't always start that way, but anything can happen on an emergency call. I'm a believer in the way you handle the calls is directly correlated to how many of these types of callers you're going to have to deal with.

Callers who feel like their emergency is being handled promptly and competently are going to be much more cooperative than callers who think you aren't listening to them, taking them seriously or getting them help quickly. My goal on every call is to keep a calm caller calm and to deescalate an agitated caller.

I reassure my callers that we are sending help several times throughout my calls. I also try to give them a reason for everything I do so they know that it's important to communicate with me. After asking them what is happening and getting my initial problem nature, I'll tell them, "I'm getting help started for you, I just need to ask you a few questions to help the responders when they arrive". After I ask the questions, I'll tell them, "The paramedics/firefighters are on their way to help you. Stay on the line and I'll tell you exactly what to do next." When I am ready to disconnect with the caller, I'll tell them again, "Help is on the way." I've found that this is a much more effective way to end the call than telling the caller we can disconnect or just saying bye.

When I need to talk to my partner, the radio operator or a supervisor, I'll tell the caller, "Hold on for just a moment while I speak to the paramedics/fire department. I'm still on the line in case anything changes." This is far more effective in keeping callers on the line and engaged than just telling them to hold on.

Of course, some calls are going to start off with a fully hysterical caller. The goal there should be able to get them to a workable level and getting the minimum amount of necessary information before trying to proceed with additional questions. Finding out their address and why they are calling should be first priority. Everybody eventually finds what works (or doesn't) for them in these situations. For some, it takes longer than others. Generally, it's not recommended to tell a caller to "calm down" or "shut up". This will just agitate them more. I try to tell hysterical callers, "Take a deep breath and talk to me so we can help the patient right now" or, "I have help on the way to you now, but I need you to work with me to help them before the responders arrive."

If someone is just out of control and you can't get any information and can't get them to help the patient/victim, there is nothing wrong with telling them to put someone else on the phone who can talk to you. Sometimes you may have to switch callers two or three times to get someone to finally step up and do CPR or provide other life-saving treatment.

Don't take it personally when they call you names or curse at you. I just ignore what they are saying in those cases and carry on like they didn't say anything. Some dispatchers will try to stop them or argue with them, but I've noticed that just makes the caller more angry or they hang up. Consider the type of person who calls for help, then takes their frustration out on the one person who is trying to help them. These people don't know you and probably (hopefully) never will, so I recommend just letting them carry on and continuing with the call as if nothing happened. You'll save a lot of your sanity this way.

MAKING PROMISES

For liability reasons, it's important that we, as dispatchers, aren't making any promises we can't deliver on. Legally, the term used is *detrimental reliance*. To summarize this term, it means that if you make a promise to a patient or caller and that promise is not delivered upon, you can be held liable because they could have otherwise pursued other means of getting help. For example, if you tell the caller that the ambulance will be there in five minutes and the crew gets diverted and it takes the cover unit an additional twenty minutes to get there, you could be held personally responsible for any deterioration in the patient's condition.

The recommended course of action in these situations is called *positive ambiguity*. Instead of telling the caller that the responders are five minutes away, I'll tell them, "They are already on their way and will be there as fast as they can." This satisfies 99% of callers who are asking how long until help arrives.

We must also be careful not to promise the callers that everything will be alright or that the patient/victim will be fine. Again, we should make ambiguous statements such as, "We're going to do this together", "You can do this" or "We're coming to help you now".

Practice making positive, yet ambiguous, statements in your daily life. People tend to react positively to these statements, without putting too many expectations on you.

SECTION III:
ZEN AND THE ART OF DISPATCH

Upon meeting a Zen master at a social event, a psychiatrist decided to ask him a question that had been on his mind. "Exactly how do you help people?" he inquired.

"I get them where they can't ask any more questions," the Master answered.

Through my martial arts practice, I've had an opportunity to study several eastern philosophies and I attempt to include them in both my practice and my daily life. I've included the explanations of some of these philosophies in this section for your reflection, meditation and amusement. I find the philosophies of Aikido to be especially useful in dispatch and in everyday conflicts. This section will begin with an explanation of what Aiki is and how I relate my understanding of it to dispatch. All of the descriptions of Aiki and Aikido are my own interpretations and are by no means a comprehensive explanation. Many other resources on Aiki are available. Some are much more sophisticated in their understanding. Others are much less enlightened. If you have an interest in this particular field of study, I recommend reading as many sources as possible, studying with experienced practitioners and forming your own opinions. A word of warning: the professed rank of a martial arts practitioner is not a reflection of their understanding of their art. Some schools (McDojos) offer black belts to anyone with a checkbook, while others save their honored ranks for the most dedicated students. I have met several nth-degree black belts who don't seem to understand Aiki at all and I've also met white belts who seem to have accepted Aiki into their spirit. Aiki and Zen can take a lifetime to master and, often, it takes several years of practice to gain an understanding of the true meaning of the practice.

The latter part of this section includes a collection of popular Zen stories. For some stories, I've made explicit correlation to aspects of our job. Others are presented without comment so you can decide on your own what it means to you and how you can relate it to your work and daily life. Some folks recommend reading Zen stories one at a time and taking time to reflect upon each of them before moving on. I recommend reading them however you feel you will get the most from it. If a story doesn't make sense to you or if you don't feel like you can relate to it, move on to another story and come back to it later. I like to read through them all and then reread them again later for new insights.

For more about using Aiki outside of the Dojo, I recommend picking up a copy of "Aikido in Everyday Life" by Terry Dobson.

AIKI, AIKIDO AND WHAT TO DO WITH IT

Aikido, or "The Peaceful Martial Art", is a Japanese martial art founded in the early 20th century by Morihei Ueshiba. It's often erroneously described as "using the attackers force against them". In my version of Aikido, the goal is not to do anything "against" anybody else. Aikido as a martial system does not include techniques found in other martial arts, such as punching and kicking. Techniques typically redirect an attack to put the attackers in a less-than advantageous position. If you'd like to read about the history of Aikido or the specific techniques, there are a plethora of books and articles out there. My goal is to talk about the philosophical aspects of Aikido and try to consolidate thousands of hours of practice over many years into just a couple of pages.

To begin with, let's talk about what the word Aikido and Aiki mean. The first character, 合 (Ai) is roughly translated as harmony, love or fitting together. If you look at the kanji (Japanese character) it represents a teapot with the lid fitting on top. The second character 気 (Ki) could be translated to mean energy or spirit. If you examine the kanji, it represents a bowl of rice with three lines of steam coming off of it. The steam represents the energy of the heat coming from the rice. Also, rice is the primary source of energy for Samurai. The final character 道 (Do) means path or way. The kanji shows a man with a hat walking down a winding path. Commonly, the translation for Aikido is given as "The way to harmonize energy". Though, you can see that it can mean other things, such as the "The path to a loving spirit". As you understand it for yourself, it will mean different things to you at different times. When I refer to Aiki, I am generally referring to the act of creating or having a harmonious spirit.

THE CIRCLE, THE SQUARE AND THE TRIANGLE

In many writings and drawings, the shapes of the circle, square and triangle are shown to represent the ideas of how energy is harmonized or redirected in Aikido. The aforementioned Terry Dobson book talks about this extensively. I'll just cover it briefly so you can see how they can relate to your callers and colleagues in dispatch.

The pointy end of the triangle represents direct energy or force. In a martial context, it would represent a direct attack from your opponent. While in dispatch, it can represent an aggressive, angry or agitated caller (or coworker).

The square is shown to represent stability. If in a fight, it would represent standing there and "taking it". For example, when a boxer is up against the ropes and he tightens his abdominal muscles while his opponent is hitting him. In everyday interaction, this could be ignoring or giving the silent treatment to someone who is being aggressive towards you. This could also be the hysterical caller on a 911 line who is unwilling or unable to communicate or act due to their panic.

Generally, the circle is the most respected shape in Aikido practice. It represents adapting, blending or redirecting energy. Often, the circle finds the path of least resistance. In martial arts, the circle can be moving around an attack and letting your opponent fly by you into the wall. In dispatch, it often involves changing tactics while speaking with callers – finding your place within their attitude and emergency.

Though the circle is highly regarded, being able to move your energy from shape to shape (shape shifting, if you will) is the pinnacle of skill. For example, if your caller is a triangle and you are a triangle, the call will often escalate and get out of control. However, if they are the triangle and you are the circle, you can find another way to calm them and get the answers that you are looking for. Then again, they may respond better if you are the square. By not responding to a callers abusive and angry comments, they may realize that their attitude is not helping them and change it. At the same time, if your caller is the square, you may need to become the triangle (at least temporarily) in order to get them to provide you with the information you need or to help the patient or victim.

Practicing these skills can help you to have easier and faster calls and lets the callers know that you are in control of the situation and they are getting the help they need. When dealing with a challenging call, try changing shapes and see if that gets you better results. With time and practice, you'll be able to easily discern which shape your caller is and which shape you need to be to best handle their emergency.

HOW TO CREATE AIKI

In Aikido, we discuss how there are four steps to creating and maintaining Aiki: Kokyu, Musubi, Awase and Zanshin.

Kokyu can be translated to mean breath. This doesn't necessarily mean breathing (although that can be a part of it). It means being centered and present yourself before you try to work outside of yourself. Feeling your feet on the ground, not being distracted by outside thoughts and being calm in your mind and breath are all part of creating good Kokyu. It should be pretty evident how being present in your own mind can make a substantial difference in the quality of calls you are taking in dispatch. There are a couple people in my communications center who seem to always be yelling at callers and having a difficult time. Knowing them personally, I'm certain it is because they lack Kokyu.

Musubi means to tie a knot. In martial arts, before practicing with someone, you need to be connected to them. You could say it's like creating Kokyu for the other person. You want to feel their feet on the ground and be connected with their energy and breath. By doing this, you can start to feel and anticipate your partners movements before they happen. Good Musubi will help you to feel and hear your caller's state of mind and be more aware of their emergency.

In Aikido, Awase is often translated as "blending". In the martial context, it's much easier to see than in the philosophical sense. When someone attacks me and I time my movements with them to get out of the way or to cause them to fall down, I am using Awase at the critical moment. In respect to dispatch, it's much harder to quantify Awase. By choosing the appropriate words and timing for the situation, you can cause your caller to be more cooperative, provide better information and to be more willing to follow your instructions. Proper Awase takes many years to master, but with practice, you can see your blending improve with each and every call.

Zanshin is the remaining mind. When you blend with your partner, you don't just let go and forget about it, you need to stay connected until the interaction is complete. In Aikido, you'll see many new students successfully throw their partner, then disconnect, think about what they just did, congratulate themselves, adjust their clothing, etc. As a student becomes more advanced, they will continue to stay connected to their partner after the Awase is complete. In the event there is another attack, they are already prepared for it. We often practice with two or three attackers in the dojo. It's important to stay connected with them at all times, as not to be dealing with just one person at a time. In dispatch, there is a lot going on. When a caller answers a question, they may give you additional information that will be valuable later. There may be other things going on in the background that you should be aware of. Additionally, you'll be interacting with other people in the dispatch center. Maintaining good Zanshin means that when you ask a question and the caller gives you an answer, you're not just focused on that one answer; you're connected through the entirety of what is happening on the callers end of the phone, as well as being able to stay connected to that caller as you handle other responsibilities.

At any point, you may need to step backward in the Aiki process. If you find yourself being distracted, it might be necessary to refocus on your Kokyu. You may need to re-tie the knot of Musubi if you are unable to stay tuned in to your caller. The point is, creating Aiki is not a 1-2-3-4 step-by-step process that is over when you get to the end. It's an organic and ever-adapting process. Great Aiki is being able to constantly adapt to any situation without losing your own Kokyu.

KICK YOU IN THE SHINS

Several traditional Japanese martial arts discuss the four minds, or Shin. It's worth noting that Shin (心) can be translated to mean either mind or heart, so if you find it more appropriate to think of these as the four hearts, please feel free. I'll use the word mind, as this is how I have learned these concepts. We've already discussed Zanshin, the remaining mind. The other three are Mushin, Fudoshin and Shoshin.

Mushin is the empty mind. This doesn't mean that you are completely without thoughts; it's being without distracting thoughts. Part of this comes with practice. Knowing your process and techniques so they are second nature will accommodate Mushin. If you are overly concerned with what you are supposed to do and what is going to happen next, you're not focusing your energy and thoughts on actually doing what you need to be doing right now. When watching martial arts masters practice, their movements and techniques seem effortless because their mind is not distracted with figuring out *what* they are going to do. Additionally, Mushin is a clear mind, the lack of the monkey mind, as it is often referred to in meditation practice. If you are thinking about your previous call, what you are going to have for dinner or that fight you had with your spouse, you are not practicing good Mushin. If this is the case, start with Kokyu and practice getting your breath and mind under control.

Fudoshin, or the immovable mind, is similar to Mushin in the respect that part of it is not being distracted with irrelevant or outside thoughts. Though, Fudoshin also means not letting yourself be disrupted. If something goes wrong, instead of allowing yourself to be flustered or frustrated, your mind can stay focused. It also means being flexible and adaptable. To compare it to martial arts, if I convince my mind that I'm going to grab my opponent and use a wrist lock on him and he counters, I can either get frustrated and continue to try repeatedly to twist his arm him without success, or I can allow myself to adapt and find the next available technique. The latter would be a more sophisticated use of Fudoshin because, even though my intention has been disrupted, I haven't allowed my mind to be distracted. Of course, more advanced practice of Mushin and Fudoshin would allow me to practice with my partner without needing to convince myself at all what I am going to do and only allowing myself to adapt to them.

  The beginner's mind, or Shoshin, is probably the easiest to learn and practice, as it can be done *after* the fact. Shoshin means allowing yourself to remember what it was like to do something for the first time – which comes in very useful when training new students or employees. It also means allowing yourself to reflect upon what you've just done with curiosity. Practicing Shoshin is not being complacent when taking your ten-thousandth call for a fall, but realizing that there is something new to be learned from each and every call. To compare it to my time as a musician, we played the same songs every night in concert and countless times in rehearsal. It became very easy to get bored of playing the same songs over and over again. One thing we must remember is that even though we may have already done it hundreds of times, for our audience, it's still new. Similarly, when taking that thousandth call for breathing problems, it's easy to be detached and bored with the same old script and same old answers. However, it's important to remember that for the caller, this may be as new as it was for you the very first time you answered a 911 line.

STORIES FROM THE MASTERS

A university professor went to visit a famous Zen master. While the master quietly served tea, the professor talked about Zen. The master poured the visitor's cup to the brim, and then kept pouring. The professor watched the overflowing cup until he could no longer restrain himself. "It's overfull! No more will go in!" the professor blurted. "You are like this cup," the master replied, "How can I show you Zen unless you first empty your cup?"

These traditional Zen stories come from various sources I've read throughout the years, as well as stories shared with me by fellow martial arts practitioners. The stories will be given *in italics* with my comments in standard font. I've only given expositions for a handful of stories, as it's up to you, the reader, to find your own lesson in these stories. I encourage you to contact me to discuss any of these ideas further.

Focus

Continuing along our path of Mushin and Fudoshin, I've here are a few stories about presence of mind and staying focused:

A first-year Aikido student approached his Sensei with a question. "I'd like to improve my knowledge

of the martial arts. In addition to learning from you, I'd like to study with another teacher in order to learn another style. What do you think of this idea?"
"The hunter who chases two rabbits," answered the Sensei, "catches neither one."

It's easy to get distracted with so much going on in the comms center. Focusing on your own call will allow you to provide the highest level of care to your caller. Try not to get yourself distracted by the call happening next to you or by thoughts of your previous calls.

After years of apprenticeship, Tenno achieved the rank of Zen teacher. One rainy day, he went to visit the famous master Nan-in. When he walked in, the master greeted him with a question, "Did you leave your shoes and umbrella on the porch?"
"Yes," Tenno replied.
"Tell me," the master continued, "did you place your umbrella to the left of your shoes, or to the right?" Tenno did not know the answer, and realized that he had not yet attained full awareness. So he became Nan-in's apprentice and studied under him for ten more years.

Seung Sahn would say, "When you eat, just eat. When you read the newspaper, just read the newspaper. Don't do anything other than what you are doing."

One day a student saw him reading the newspaper while he was eating. The student asked if this did not contradict his teachings.
Seung Sahn said, "When you eat and read the newspaper, just eat and read the newspaper."

"Why must I meditate in order to achieve enlightenment?" demanded the prince of his teacher. "I can study. I can pray. I can think on issues clearly. Why this silly emptying of the mind?"
"I will show you," said the teacher, taking a bucket of water into the garden under the full moon. "Now I stir the surface and what do you see?"
"Ribbons of light," answered the prince.
"Now wait," said the teacher setting the bucket down.
Both teacher and boy watched the calming surface of the water in the bamboo bucket for many minutes.
"Now what do you see?" asked the teacher.
"The moon," replied the prince.
"So, too, young master, the only way to grasp enlightenment is through a calm and settled mind"

The students in the monastery were in total awe of the elder monk, not because he was strict, but because nothing ever seemed to upset or ruffle him. So they found him a bit unearthly and even frightening. One day they decided to put him to a test. A bunch of them very quietly hid in a dark corner of one of the hallways, and waited for the monk to walk by. Within moments, the old man appeared, carrying a cup of hot tea. Just as he passed by, the students all rushed out at him screaming as loud as they could. But the monk showed no reaction whatsoever. He peacefully made his way to a small table at the end of the hall, gently placed the cup down, and then, leaning against the wall, cried out with shock, "Ohhhhh!"

Adaptability

A little bear cub was confused about how to walk. "What do I do first?" he asked his mother. "Do I start with my right foot or my left? Or both front feet and then my back feet? Or do I move both feet on one side and then both feet on the other?"
His mother answered, "Just quit thinking and start walking."

A Taoist story tells of an old man who accidentally fell into the river rapids leading to a high and dangerous waterfall. Onlookers feared for his life. Miraculously, he came out alive and unharmed downstream at the bottom of the falls. People asked him how he managed to survive. "I accommodated myself to the water, not the water to me. Without thinking, I allowed myself to be shaped by it. Plunging into the swirl, I came out with the swirl. This is how I survived."

Often, when training new call-takers, I find them getting frustrated when the caller is not answering their questions quickly and concisely. I have to regularly remind them that their job is not to take over the emergency, but to fit into it. It's one thing to take control of the call and another to make it all about you. Always remember, you aren't the one having the emergency.

A student went to his meditation teacher and said, "My meditation is horrible! I feel so distracted, or my legs ache, or I'm constantly falling asleep. It's just horrible!"
"It will pass," the teacher said matter-of-factly.
A week later, the student came back to his teacher. "My meditation is wonderful! I feel so aware, so peaceful and so alive! It's just wonderful!'
"It will pass," the teacher replied matter-of-factly.

Two traveling monks reached a river where they met a young woman. Wary of the current, she asked if they could carry her across. One of the monks hesitated, but the other quickly picked her up onto his shoulders, transported her across the water, and put her down on the other bank. She thanked him and departed. As the monks continued on their way, one was brooding and preoccupied. Unable to hold his silence, he spoke out. "Brother, our spiritual training teaches us to avoid any

contact with women, but you picked that one up on your shoulders and carried her!"
"Brother," the second monk replied, "I set her down on the other side, while you are still carrying her."

Each call will end and we will eventually hang up. Much of the stress that dispatchers suffer from comes from holding on to their calls after they hang up.

The purpose of a fish trap is to catch fish, and when the fish are caught, the trap is forgotten.
The purpose of a rabbit snare is to catch rabbits. When the rabbits are caught, the snare is forgotten.
The purpose of words is to convey ideas. When the ideas are grasped, the words are forgotten.
Where can I find a man who has forgotten words? He is the one I would like to talk to.

There is a story of an old farmer who had worked his crops for many years. One day his horse ran away. Upon hearing the news, his neighbors came to visit. "Such bad luck," they said sympathetically.
"May be," the farmer replied.
The next morning the horse returned, bringing with it three other wild horses. "How wonderful," the neighbors exclaimed.
"May be," replied the old man.
The following day, his son tried to ride one of the untamed horses, was thrown, and broke his leg.

The neighbors again came to offer their sympathy on his misfortune.
"May be," answered the farmer.
The day after, military officials came to the village to draft young men into the army. Seeing that the son's leg was broken, they passed him by. The neighbors congratulated the farmer on how well things had turned out.
"May be," said the farmer.

A beautiful girl in the village was pregnant. Her angry parents demanded to know who the father was. At first resistant to confess, the anxious and embarrassed girl finally pointed to Hakuin, the Zen master whom everyone previously revered for living such a pure life. When the outraged parents confronted Hakuin with their daughter's accusation, he simply replied "Is that so?"
When the child was born, the parents brought it to the Hakuin, who now was viewed as a pariah by the whole village. They demanded that he take care of the child since it was his responsibility. "Is that so?" Hakuin said calmly as he accepted the child.
For many months he took very good care of the child until the daughter could no longer withstand the lie she had told. She confessed that the real father was a young man in the village whom she had tried to protect. The parents immediately went to Hakuin to see if he would return the baby. With profuse apologies they explained what had

happened. "Is that so?" Hakuin said as he handed them the child.

Communication

We deal with a lot of different personalities every day. We have irate callers, panicked callers, intoxicated callers, five-year-old callers and little old lady callers. Each and every caller is going to behave differently. While practicing Aiki, we are adapting ourselves to each caller and situation. Unfortunately, some of the most difficult personalities we are going to deal with every day are our co-workers. Hopefully, these stories will help us learn more about ourselves and how we deal with both our colleagues and our callers.

In ancient times it was customary for a traveling monk seeking lodging at a Zen monastery to engage in dharma combat with the head monk. If the wayfarer won the debate, he could stay; if not, he had to seek quarters elsewhere.
Once, a master assigned his attendant to engage in such an encounter with a traveling monk, who challenged him to a silent debate. It so happened that this attendant had but one eye.
Soon the wayfarer returned to the master, saying, "Your man is too good for me. I must journey on. I held up one finger to symbolize the Buddha. But he held up two fingers for the Buddha and the Dharma.

So I held up three fingers for the Buddha, the Dharma and the Sangha. But then he held up a clenched fist to indicate they were all one - I am no match for him."

When the traveler who spoke these words left, the attendant arrived - angry and out of breath. "Where is that rascal?" he demanded. "First, he insulted me by holding up one finger to indicate I had only one eye. Determined to be polite in spite of that, I held up two fingers to indicate that, on the other hand, he was blessed with two eyes. But he just kept rubbing it in, for next he held up three fingers to indicate that all together there were only three eyes among us. So I went to hit him and he ran off! Where is he hiding?"

Like the silent debate in these stories, as dispatchers we are lacking a major aspect of communication. We are unable to use body language with our callers, which makes it even more important that we pay close attention to not only what we are saying, but how we say it.

A blind man who lived near the master's temple told a friend: "Since I am blind, I cannot watch a person's face, so I must judge his character by the sound of his voice. Ordinarily, when I hear someone congratulate another upon his happiness or success, I also hear a secret tone of envy. When condolence is expressed for the misfortune of another, I hear pleasure and satisfaction, as if the one condoling was really glad there was something left to gain in his own world. In all my experience, however, the master's voice was always sincere. Whenever he expressed happiness, I heard nothing but happiness, and whenever he expressed sorrow, sorrow was all I heard."

There once lived a great warrior. Though quite old, he still was able to defeat any challenger. His reputation extended far and wide throughout the land and many students gathered to study under him. One day an infamous young warrior arrived at the village. He was determined to be the first man to defeat the great master. Along with his strength, he had an uncanny ability to spot and exploit any weakness in an opponent. He would wait for his opponent to make the first move, thus revealing a weakness, and then would strike with merciless force and lightning speed. No one had ever lasted with him in a match beyond the first move. Much against the advice of his concerned students, the old master gladly accepted the young warrior's challenge. As the two squared off for battle, the young warrior began to hurl insults at the old master. He threw dirt and spit in his face. For hours he verbally assaulted him with every curse and insult known to mankind. But the old warrior merely stood there motionless and calm. Finally, the young warrior exhausted himself. Knowing he was defeated, he left feeling shamed. Somewhat disappointed that he did not fight the insolent youth, the students gathered around the old master and questioned him. "How could you endure such an indignity? How did you drive him away?"

"If someone comes to give you a gift and you do not receive it," the master replied, "to whom does the gift belong?"

Two monks were washing their bowls in the river when they noticed a scorpion that was drowning. One monk immediately scooped it up and set it upon the bank. In the process he was stung. He went back to washing his bowl and again the scorpion fell in. The monk saved the scorpion and was again stung. The other monk asked him, "Friend, why do you continue to save the scorpion when you know its nature is to sting?"

"Because," the monk replied, "to save it is my nature."

A farmer whose corn always took the first prize at the state fair had a habit of sharing his best corn seed with all the farmers in the neighborhood.

When asked why, he said, "It is really a matter of self-interest. The wind picks up the pollen and carries it from field to field. So if my neighbors grow inferior corn, the cross-pollination brings down the quality of my own corn. That is why I am concerned that they plant only the very best."

A great festival was to be held in a village and each villager was asked to contribute by pouring a bottle of wine into a giant barrel. One of the villagers had this thought: "If I pour a bottle of water in that giant barrel, no one will notice the difference." But it didn't occur to him that everyone else in the village might have the same thought. When the banquet began and the barrel was tapped, what came out was pure water.

What does integrity mean to you? Are you helping others by sharing your corn, or are you pouring water into the wine barrel?

There once was a monastery that was very strict. Following a vow of silence, no one was allowed to speak at all. But there was one exception to this rule. Every ten years, the monks were permitted to speak just two words. After spending his first ten years at the monastery, one monk went to the head monk. "It has been ten years," said the head monk. "What are the two words you would like to speak?"
"Bed... hard..." said the monk.
"I see," replied the head monk.
Ten years later, the monk returned to the head monk's office. "It has been ten more years," said the head monk. "What are the two words you would like to speak?"
"Food... stinks..." said the monk.
"I see," replied the head monk.

Yet another ten years passed and the monk once again met with the head monk who asked, "What are your two words now, after these ten years?"
"I... quit!" said the monk.
"Well, I can see why," replied the head monk. "All you ever do is complain."

An aging master grew tired of his apprentice complaining, and so, one morning, he sent him for some salt. When the apprentice returned, the master instructed the unhappy young man to put a handful of salt in a glass of water and then to drink it.
"How does it taste?" the master asked.
"Bitter," spit the apprentice.
The master chuckled and then asked the young man to take the same handful of salt and put it in the lake. The two walked in silence to the nearby lake, and once the apprentice swirled his handful of salt in the water, the old man said, "Now drink from the lake."
As the water dripped down the young man's chin, the master asked, "How does it taste?"
"Much fresher," remarked the apprentice.
"Do you taste the salt?" asked the master.
"No," said the young man.
At this, the master sat beside the young man who so reminded him of himself and took his hands, offering, "The pain of life is pure salt, no more, no less. The amount of pain in life remains the same, exactly the same. But the amount of bitterness we

taste depends on the container we put the pain in. So when you are in pain, the only thing you can do is to enlarge your sense of things... Stop being a glass. Become a lake."

A group of frogs were traveling through the woods, when two of them fell into a deep pit. All the other frogs gathered around the pit. When they saw how deep it was, they told the two frogs that they were as good as dead.
The two frogs ignored the comments and tried to jump up out of the pit with all of their might. The other frogs kept telling them to stop, that they were as good as dead.
Finally, one of the frogs took heed to what the other frogs were saying and gave up. She fell down and died. The other frog continued to jump as hard as she could. Once again, the crowd of frogs yelled at her to stop the pain and just die. She began jumping even harder and finally made it out. When she got out, the other frogs said, "Did you not hear us?" The frog explained to them that she was deaf - she thought they were encouraging her to jump out of the hole the entire time.

The master Bankei's talks were attended not only by Zen students but by persons of all ranks and sects. He never quoted sutras, nor indulged in scholastic dissertations. Instead, his words were spoken directly from his heart to the hearts of his listeners. His large audience angered a priest of the

Nichiren sect because the adherents had left to hear about Zen. The self-centered Nichiren priest came to the temple, determined to have a debate with Bankei. "Hey, Zen teacher!" he called out. "Wait a minute. Whoever respects you will obey what you say, but a man like myself does not respect you. Can you make me obey you?"
"Come up beside me and I will show you," said Bankei.
Proudly the priest pushed his way through the crowd to the teacher. Bankei smiled. "Come over to my left side." The priest obeyed.
"No," said Bankei, "we may talk better if you are on the right side. Step over here." The priest proudly stepped over to the right.
"You see," observed Bankei, "you are obeying me and I think you are a very gentle person. Now sit down and listen."

Humility

Word spread across the countryside about the wise Holy Man who lived in a small house atop the mountain. A man from the village decided to make the long and difficult journey to visit him. When he arrived at the house, he saw an old servant inside who greeted him at the door. "I would like to see the wise Holy Man," he said to the servant. The servant smiled and led him inside. As they walked through the house, the man from the village looked eagerly around the house, anticipating his encounter with the Holy Man. Before he knew it, he had been led to the back door and escorted outside. He stopped and turned to the servant, "But I want to see the Holy Man!"

"You already have," said the old man. "Everyone you may meet in life, even if they appear plain and insignificant... see each of them as a wise Holy Man. If you do this, then whatever problem you brought here today will be solved."

Once a group of beggars afflicted with leprosy came to the assembly of a Zen master, a great-hearted teacher of the masses. The master admitted them to his company, and when he initiated them, he even washed and shaved their heads with his own hands.

There was a gentleman present, the representative of a baron who had already built a temple in his province where the teacher could train disciples and lecture to the people.

Revolted by the sight of the Zen master shaving the heads of untouchables, the gentleman hurriedly brought a basin of water for the master to wash his hands. But the master refused, remarking, "Your disgust is filthier than their sores."

When speaking to your callers, are you judging them by the neighborhood they are calling from or their accent? Or are you dealing with each caller with the same respect and providing them an equal level of care?

Wealthy patrons invited Ikkyu to a banquet. Ikkyu arrived dressed in his beggar's robes. The host, not recognizing him, chased him away.

Ikkyu went home, changed into his ceremonial robe of purple brocade, and returned.

With great respect, he was received into the banquet room. There, he put his robe on the cushion, saying, "Evidently you invited the robe since you showed me away a little while ago," and left.

One day there was an earthquake that shook the entire Zen temple. Parts of it even collapsed. Many of the monks were terrified. When the earthquake stopped the teacher said, "Now you have had the opportunity to see how a Zen man behaves in a crisis situation. You may have noticed that I did not panic. I was quite aware of what was happening and what to do. I led you all to the kitchen, the strongest part of the temple. It was a good decision, because you see we have all survived without any injuries. However, despite my self-control and composure, I did feel a little bit tense - which you may have deduced from the fact that I drank a large glass of water, something I never do under ordinary circumstances."

One of the monks smiled, but didn't say anything.

"What are you laughing at?" asked the teacher.

"That wasn't water," the monk replied, *"It was a large glass of soy sauce."*

Four monks decided to meditate silently without speaking for two weeks. By nightfall on the first day, the candle began to flicker and then went out. The first monk said, "Oh, no! The candle is out."
The second monk said, "Aren't we not supposed to talk?"
The third monk said, "Why must you two break the silence?"
The fourth monk laughed and said, "Ha! I'm the only one who didn't speak."

In the communications center, there may be many individuals who think of themselves as "better" dispatchers than their colleagues – mostly based on the "I was here first" mentality. They may think they know everything there is to know. These individuals lack Shoshin and may not be the best examples to model yourself after.

"When you have a talking mouth, you have no listening ears. When you have listening ears, you have no talking mouth. Think about this carefully."

"Do not consider yourself elevated in comparison to ordinary people. Those who are commonplace just

rise and fall on the road of fame and profit, without practicing the Way or following the Way.

"They are only to be pitied, not despised or resented. Do not give rise to judgmental thoughts by comparing yourself to them: do not give rise to ideas of higher and lower.

"This is the attitude needed to enter the Way of the sages and saints, Buddhas and bodhisattvas. Therefore we place ourselves in the state of ordinary people, assimilating to the ordinary, while our will is on the Way, and we investigate its wonders."

I went to meditate on the outskirts of my ranch. Now, it so happened that there was a cowboy in the corral beating a horse. Seeing this, I hollered, "Hey! What do you think you are doing?"
This happened three times before the cowboy stopped and got off his horse. Approaching me, the cowboy said, "You were yelling at me. Do you have something to tell me?"
I replied, "Rather than beat your horse for being unruly, why not chastise yourself and train your own mind right?"

One day Chuang Tzu and a friend were walking by a river. "Look at the fish swimming about," said Chuang Tzu, "They are really enjoying themselves."
"You are not a fish," replied the friend, "So you can't truly know that they are enjoying themselves."

"You are not me," said Chuang Tzu. "So how do you know that I do not know that the fish are enjoying themselves?"

Other Assorted Stories

When the spiritual teacher and his disciples began their evening meditation, the cat who lived in the monastery made such noise that it distracted them. So the teacher ordered that the cat be tied up during the evening practice. Years later, when the teacher died, the cat continued to be tied up during the meditation session. And when the cat eventually died, another cat was brought to the monastery and tied up. Centuries later, learned descendants of the spiritual teacher wrote scholarly treatises about the religious significance of tying up a cat for meditation practice.

Oftentimes, we have so many policies and procedures to follow, we lose sight of what our real goals are. When taking calls, if you find that things can be done another, more efficient way, speak up. You might be the one to change the policies and improve the entire agency or industry.

A martial arts student went to his teacher and said earnestly, "I am devoted to studying your martial system. How long will it take me to master it?"
The teacher's reply was casual, "Ten years."

Impatiently, the student answered, "But I want to master it faster than that. I will work very hard. I will practice every day, ten or more hours a day if I have to. How long will it take then?"
The teacher thought for a moment, "20 years."

When we set our intention on a specific goal – a promotion or recognition – we give up being present in what we are doing right now.

The master at the school for archery was known to be a master of life just as much as of archery. One day his brightest pupil scored three bull's-eyes in a row at a local contest. Everyone went wild with applause. Congratulations poured in for pupil -- and master. The master, however, seemed unimpressed -- almost critical even.
When the pupil later asked him why, he said, "You have yet to learn that the target is not the target."

One day a young Buddhist on his journey home, came to the banks of a wide river.
Staring hopelessly at the great obstacle in front of him, he pondered for hours on just how to cross such a wide barrier. Just as he was about to give up his pursuit to continue his journey he saw a great teacher on the other side of the river. The young Buddhist yells over to the teacher, "Oh wise one, can you tell me how to get to the other side of this river?" The teacher ponders for a moment

looks up and down the river and yells back, "My son, you are on the other side."

A story tells of a man who prayed continually for the awareness to succeed in life. Then one night he dreamed of going into the forest to attain understanding. The next morning he went into the woods and wandered for several hours looking for some sign that would provide answers. When he finally stopped to rest, he saw a fox with no legs lying between two rocks in a cool place.

Curious as to how a legless fox could survive, he waited until sunset when he observed a lion come and lay meat before the fox. "Ah, I understand," the man thought. "The secret to success in life is to trust that God will take care of all my needs. I don't need to provide for myself. All I have to do is totally surrender to my all-sustaining God."

Two weeks later, weakened and starving, the man had another dream. In it he heard a voice say, "Fool. Be like the lion, not like the fox."

Late one night a blind man was about to go home after visiting a friend. "Please," he said to his friend, "may I take your lantern with me?"

"Why carry a lantern?" asked his friend. "You won't see any better with it."

"No," said the blind one, "perhaps not. But others will see me better, and not bump into me." So his friend gave the blind man the lantern, which was

made of paper and bamboo strips, with a candle inside.
Off went the blind man with the lantern, and before he had gone more than a few yards, *Crack!* - a traveler walked right into him. The blind man was very angry. "Why don't you look out?" he stormed. "Don't you see this lantern?"
"Why don't you light the candle?" asked the traveler.

Two men, both seriously ill, occupied the same hospital room. One man was allowed to sit up in his bed for an hour each afternoon to help drain the fluid from his lungs. His bed was next to the room's only window. The other man had to spend all his time flat on his back. The men talked for hours on end. They spoke of their wives and families, their homes, their jobs, their involvement in the military service, where they had been on vacation. And every afternoon when the man in the bed by the window could sit up, he would pass the time by describing to his room-mate all the things he could see outside the window.
The man in the other bed began to live for those one-hour periods where his world would be broadened and enlivened by all the activity and color of the world outside. The window overlooked a park with a lovely lake. Ducks and swans played on the water while children sailed their model boats. Young lovers walked arm in arm amidst flowers of every color of the rainbow. Grand old trees graced

the landscape, and a fine view of the city skyline could be seen in the distance. As the man by the window described all this in exquisite detail, the man on the other side of the room would close his eyes and imagine the picturesque scene.

One warm afternoon the man by the window described a parade passing by. Although the other man couldn't hear the band -- he could see it in his mind's eye as the gentleman by the window portrayed it with descriptive words. Then unexpectedly, a sinister thought entered his mind; why should the other man alone experience all the pleasures of seeing everything while he himself never got to see anything? It didn't seem fair.

At first thought the man felt ashamed. But as the days passed and he missed seeing more sights, he allowed his envy to erode into resentment and it soon turned him sour. He began to brood and he found himself unable to sleep. He should be by that window -- that thought, and only that thought now controlled his life.

Late one night as he lay staring at the ceiling, the man by the window began to cough. He was choking on the fluid in his lungs. The other man watched in the dimly lit room as the struggling man by the window groped for the button to call for help. Listening from across the room he never moved, never pushed his own button which would have brought the nurse running in. In less than five minutes the coughing and choking stopped, along with that the sound of breathing. Now there was only silence -- deathly silence.

The following morning the day nurse arrived to bring water for their baths. When she found the lifeless body of the man by the window, she was saddened and called the hospital attendants to take it away.
As soon as it seemed appropriate, the other man asked if he could be moved next to the window. The nurse was happy to make the switch, and after making sure he was comfortable, she left him alone. Slowly, painfully, he propped himself up on one elbow to take his first look at the world outside. Finally, he would have the joy of seeing it all himself. He strained to slowly turn to look out the window beside the bed.
It faced a blank wall!
The man asked the nurse what could have compelled his deceased roommate who had described such wonderful things outside this window. The nurse responded that the man was blind and could not even see the wall. She said, "Perhaps he just wanted to encourage you."

Soyen Shaku, the first Zen teacher to come to America, said: "My heart burns like fire but my eyes are as cold as dead ashes." He made the following rules which he practiced every day of his life:
In the morning before dressing, light incense and meditate.
Retire at a regular hour.
Partake of food at regular intervals.

Eat with moderation and never to the point of satisfaction.
Receive a guest with the same attitude you have when alone. When alone, maintain the same attitude you have in receiving guests.
Watch what you say, and whatever you say, practice it.
When an opportunity comes do not let it pass you by, yet always think twice before acting.
Do not regret the past. Look to the future.
Have the fearless attitude of a hero and the loving heart of a child.
Upon retiring, sleep as if you had entered your last sleep. Upon awakening, leave your bed behind you instantly as if you had cast away a pair of old shoes.

**SECTION IV:
CONSOLE CHRONICLES**

In our busy call center, we receive over a thousand EMS and fire calls every day. Personally, I average about one hundred calls each day. The vast majority of these calls are the same from day to day – falls, breathing problems, chest pains and countless calls from medical facilities and convalescent homes. After a while, they all start to blend together; most days when I get home I can't remember any of the calls I took that day. When I had the idea for this book, I started writing myself little notes about any particularly interesting calls to help me remember. Even then, I'm still only able to remember the details from a handful of calls. I've asked a few of my fellow dispatchers to include some of their memorable calls as well. I let them know that the calls could be anything they found particularly challenging, educational or funny. I've credited them either by name or anonymously, at their request.

Dispatchers with stories they would like to share are encouraged to email me for inclusion in a future edition.

"Thank God we took a mule with us on the picnic because when one of the boys was injured we used the mule to carry him back."
"How did he get injured?"
"The mule kicked him."

A young woman in her twenties called 911 one Friday evening to let us know that the mosquitoes wouldn't stop biting her. After the initial questioning, she admitted she was drunk and stoned, sitting outside on her back patio under the porch lights. It would have made more sense to tell her to go inside and close the door – but since she was calling for an ambulance, she got one.

A woman in her eighties called one afternoon for an ambulance because her husband was outside and had been bitten by a tick.

I received a call from a lady one morning who went on in great detail about not being able to poop for several days. She was sitting on the toilet, trying to go at the time. A couple of minutes into the call, I heard the most painful, blood-curdling screams. This went on for about ninety seconds. I kept asking her what was happening, but she wouldn't answer me. I was beginning to wonder if I should get PD started for a murder in progress. Then she came back on the phone and requested to cancel the ambulance.

A homeless lady called from the side of the canal, saying she was shitting herself. She began yelling, "It's pouring out". I had a trainee at the time and the rest of us had a lot of fun answering the questions she was asking the patient. "What color clothes are you wearing?" "Shit colored".

In a less-than-savory neighborhood, a young woman calls 911 and when I ask her "Tell me exactly what happened" she goes into a tirade about how she doesn't need our help and we always call her a crackhead – she's not a crackhead, I'm an asshole, etc. Needless-to-say, she got help from both the psychiatric unit and the police.

PD transferred over a call and after providing the address to the patient at Walgreens, she said, "Go ahead, ma'am". I was greeted with yelling about "I'm an Italian fucking man, stop calling me ma'am". My response: "Hello, sir, what are your closest cross streets".

An example of how accents can make all the difference in speedy response: A caller with a heavy Indian accent tells me she is at Simone and Fowler. Fowler is one of the major streets in our area, so I put it in, the cross-streets verify and I get the unit rolling. Seems suspicious, as she is pinging nowhere near there. It happens - maybe she's calling for someone else or the ping is way off. I ask her what city she's in and she says Sanger. The location I have is in a city over twenty miles away –

coincidentally *in* Fowler. After some extensive searching, I discovered that there is a Simone and FALLER street in Sanger!

In a related issue, why does every city in a three county area need to name their streets the same?!? Do we not have enough Olives and Inyos and Tuolumnes and Merceds in one city? Don't even get me started on the numbered and lettered streets.

A frantic, crying young mother calls 911 in a panic. I immediately think it's going to be for a choking or febrile seizure, as those callers are almost always a mess. After calming her down enough to understand at least a portion of what she is saying, I learn that her baby somehow got a hair wrapped around her toe and the toe was turning purple. I guess she didn't own a pair of scissors.

In one of my all-time favorite calls, the employees of one of the local USPS offices call 911. After verifying the address, I ask them to tell me exactly what happened. The employee tells me the story about how the manager had smashed her finger in the safe. I put the call in for a traumatic injury and start the ambulance and fire department. The next question I ask is "Are you with the patient now". The employee seems bewildered and explains to me (like I should already know) that someone else drove the manager to the hospital.

By now, I'm really confused, so I ask the caller, "Ooookay, why did you need an ambulance?"
"Well, we found the finger and we wanted you to come pick it up and take it to the hospital." Ummm...that's probably not going to happen, but I ask my supervisor and he tells me that we won't come get the finger. I advise the caller and let him know that somebody there needs to get a bag or an envelope and take the finger to the hospital. He says that nobody there wants to touch it. They even called in the janitor but he wouldn't do it either. I can only imagine the medics showing up, strapping the finger to the gurney, putting the oxygen on it and wheeling it into the back of the rig. I probably should have told them to mail it (or send it UPS if they wanted it to actually get there).

Me: "Tell me exactly what happened". Old lady: "My butt fell out while I was pooping."

I don't let a lot of calls get to me. With all of the death and violence I'm exposed to, it's few and far between that a call bothers me while I'm on the phone or after I hang up. I took a call one afternoon for a sick person - no priority symptoms, just not feeling well. After I talked to her for a little while, she told me that she is too sick to work as a teacher because of her alcoholism. Her children don't talk to her and she is basically dying due to her addiction. The whole time, she keeps saying that she felt bad for calling because she doesn't have a "real" emergency. I continued to reassure her that she was doing the right thing and we were here to help. No telling why, but that call made me sad.

In a similar story, a woman in her nineties called in because she thought he had another stroke. I told her I was getting help started and she told me that she was ready to die and to just let her die. She told me how she had no family, had CHF, among other issues and didn't want to live any more. I stayed on the phone with her for the seven minutes that it took for help to arrive, reassuring her that we didn't want her to die and that the medics were going to be there soon to help her. For all I know, she probably is dead by now. Or worse, in a convalescent home.

A relatively calm lady calls in to tell us about how a tree fell on her husband. Judging by the tone in her voice, it doesn't sound serious - maybe some cuts and bruises or a broken leg, right? I go through the standard questioning. A few questions in, she gets suddenly agitated and begins screaming, "The tree fell on him and he's dead! He's broken in half! He's smashed!"

In one of the strangest calls I've ever received, an obviously drunk or altered man calls for an ambulance, saying he is in Fresno at the corner of Jensen and Elm. The call comes in through Tulare County and he is pinging in Tulare. That's not unprecedented. The GPS sometimes does weird things. So I send the ambulance out to Jensen and Elm. The caller is walking down the street at the time and, typically, with callers who are moving, I'll stay on the phone until crews arrive to make sure they can find him. Crews arrive and, of course, can't find him. He confirms, again and again, that he is at that intersection in Fresno. I begin asking him for landmarks, he says that he's by a building that sells oxygen cylinders and gives the name of the brand on the banner. He also says he walked by Clinica Sierra Vista a few minutes ago. Sure enough, I look on street view and I find the clinic and the oxygen place right at the intersection of Jensen and Elm. Crews still can't find him. He says a bus is passing by and says its bus 32. I check the city website for bus routes and find that bus 32 goes right by that intersection. At this point, I'm trying to figure out exactly where he is. The crews are driving around every parking lot in the area, looking for him. I ask the crews to start chirping their siren so I can hear if they are nearby. They do and I hear nothing in the background. At this point, the call has been going on for almost twenty minutes. I'm at a loss. I've re-pinged his GPS several times and every time he is coming up in Tulare. I decide to open up street view for where he is pinging. Unbelievably, I find an oxygen place with the same banner and a clinic right where he was pinging. So, after all that, he was exactly where the GPS said he was.

A guy is walking down the street when a passing car either shoots him or throws something at him and hits him in the back of the head. When PD sends it over to me, they say it was something thrown - probably because they don't want to respond. Either way, this guy is out of it. Due to drugs or the head injury, I don't know. He has no idea where he is. Based on his GPS, I have a general vicinity. He can't tell me any of the street signs near him or any landmarks, except that he is by a lake. He's in the middle of the city and we don't have lakes. I'm thinking that he's by a ponding basin and start crews that direction. As is usual for these situations, he doesn't just stop on a street corner and wait, he keeps walking. I have my intern, AJ, keep him talking while I try to communicate with PD and get a better GPS location. This is the first time AJ has had to deal with this kind of situation and doesn't know exactly what to say. I tell him to just keep the caller talking about anything - sports, TV, whatever. AJ asks the caller if he watches TV and what he likes, which was a good choice because the caller has a lot of opinions about TV. He goes on to tell us how good he is at picking out TV shows and he knows the best shows. After a while of searching around for him, he gets suddenly weak and keeps saying how bad he needs water. Reminds me of those Vietnam movies where the dying soldiers are begging for water. We convince him to stop and sit down on the curb and we will bring him water. Due to the volatile nature of the situation, we have PD out looking for the subject. He sees the police, but doesn't want to talk to them and he is hiding behind a parked car. We finally convince him that the police are there to bring him water and he reveals himself. I never did find out if it was a gunshot or not. I did, however, learn that the best show on TV is Real Husbands of Hollywood.

Technically, when someone eats pot edibles and calls 911, it would be considered Overdose/Poisoning. Seems a little extreme. In the case of the 55-year old woman who called me one night, she definitely needed help as quickly as I could get it to her. In order to treat her fibromyalgia, she decided to try edibles. She told me in her whole life she had never smoked a joint or a cigarette. She stared with one square of a chocolate bar. By the time she got on the phone with me, she was in full-blown panic mode. Afraid she was going to die, having breathing problems. I didn't think it would be appropriate to tell her that it happens to everyone their first time and she should just get some Funyuns and chill.

Sometimes the callers just aren't clear about what's happening and it leads to a situation getting a little out of control. An office administrator at a local elementary school called 911 one morning just after I'd cleared to work on my own. When I asked the caller to tell me what happened, she said there was a second-grader outside who was on a tower and threatening to jump. She's in the office and not with the patient at the time, so it's difficult to get any additional details. Our typical response to someone threatening to jump are three fire apparatus, the jump bag, the EMS rescue unit and the police. So I roll them all that direction. The first engine to the scene radios in stating that they don't see any towers near the school. I'm on street view trying to find a nearby tower. There's a water tower a few blocks away, but the caller said the patient was out behind the school in the field area. The engine gets waved in by the school maintenance and directed to the patient. He was about seven feet up a playground slide tower, not wanting to come in from recess. They cancelled the jump bag.

When I was training, my preceptor was a former medic and, like me, isn't grossed out by much. In the four weeks we spent together, she had to take off her headset once. We received a call from an elderly, disabled man living in a slum hotel in Hanford. Coincidentally, she knew this patient from her time as a medic. He proceeded to tell us about how he was infested with bugs. They were in his beard and eyebrows, under his fingernails and all over his bed. I didn't find it that gross, so I kept him on the phone and let him keep telling me about it - mostly just to gross out my preceptor.

In one of my most difficult calls as a trainee, a one-year old had been playing outside with his four-year old cousin unattended. The four-year old came in and told the parents that the baby had fallen into a bucket. It was winter and there had been a lot of rain lately. By the time I got the call, the baby was in full arrest. The mother was screaming hysterically and was of no help either answering questions or starting resuscitation. Fortunately, I was able to have her pass the phone off to the child's aunt who, although I was unable to hear her over the mother's screaming, managed to follow my CPR instructions. We did CPR for over ten minutes, since the call was in a rural area. The crews arrived and took over and they air-lifted the baby to the nearest base hospital. According to the local news when I left that evening the baby was pronounced dead. I received several text messages later that evening from my colleagues that the news had retracted their story and the baby was alive. As far as I know, the child made a full recovery.

Sometimes, when it rains, it pours. We're a high-volume call center, taking approximately 1,000 calls per day. I've noticed a trend of similar calls on particular days. If it's hot and dry outside, it might be an outside fire day. If it's cold and rainy out, it'll be COPD day. Some days are psychiatric days, some are rectal bleed days and others are callers-who-don't-know-their-address days. One day, just for me, it was cardiac arrest day. I was on the 5 am shift at the time and within my first hour of work, I had three cardiacs. Continuing the trend, I took a total of nine cardiacs that day. One was my first confirmed save. The other eight, I'll never know.

Inevitably, when it's ten minutes until end of shift, someone is going to go into cardiac arrest and they will most certainly be thirty miles from the nearest ambulance post. I've had several long CPR calls but one in particular holds the record. A gentleman and his boss were enjoying some barbeque on the back porch of the latter's mountain home when he began to choke and became unconscious. Since we don't perform the Heimlich on unconscious patients, I had the caller begin CPR. Although the ambulance was coming from the next mountain town over, there was a local volunteer firefighter company just down the street from this address. We worked CPR on this patient for about ten minutes while our unit was en route, but still hadn't heard anything from fire dispatch. I asked the radio operator to call CDF and find out when fire would be there. We eventually heard back from them that they had a ten minute ETA. By this time, we were about twenty minutes into the call.

Another ten minutes later, our ambulance arrived with fire still nowhere in sight. The poor caller worked CPR for the full thirty minutes without stopping. Unfortunately, the patient didn't make it.

It was my first Thanksgiving in dispatch. I received a call from a lady who was slurring-drunk and saying she wanted to kill herself. She admitted that she had already consumed a whole bottle of vodka. It was just after 11 am at this point. Initially, she was sitting on the front porch of her house in a relatively affluent neighborhood - as affluent as Fresno can get, I guess. Our typical response for psychiatric issues with no priority symptoms is priority 3, no lights and sirens. While waiting for the crews to arrive, she decided she didn't want to be around the house and started walking. Unfortunately, she was too disoriented to know where she was walking and I could only understand about a third of what she was saying. I was desperately trying to get her to give me names off of street signs, business names or anything I could pass on to the radio op. Finally, she saw a liquor store and said she was going to get more vodka. Unlike most neighborhoods in Fresno, there's not a liquor store on every corner in her neighborhood. She told me the liquor store was next to a donut shop and I was able to find it on my map and get the crews headed in the right direction. Meanwhile, I was able to convince her to not get another bottle of vodka and wait outside. Hopefully she had a better Christmas.

I came into work on New Year's Day at 5 am and one of the first calls I got was from a young lady who said her roommate was having a mental breakdown. From the sound of things, he had probably been out drinking and doing drugs since the night before. She was trying to be discreet with her call and was hiding in her room. I tried to get her to leave and go wait outside or in her car, but she didn't want him to get suspicious. He was acting unpredictably and I was worried about violence, so I decided to stay on the phone with her while waiting for PD to show up. It took them about thirty minutes. I heard all about her personal life and problems. Every three or four minutes, the patient would be banging on her door and yelling at her. I found out they had just moved in together a couple of days prior and hadn't unpacked yet. At one point, while he was yelling at her, I heard her say, "Just because I fucked you doesn't mean I want to be with you and I don't owe you anything". Eventually the cops showed up and everyone was safe. The moral of the story is: don't move in with some crazy person you just hooked up with.

The amount of pain and the caller's reaction is not always (and usually not) indicative of the severity of injuries. One early, rainy morning I received a 911 call from a young man who had taken the corner at the freeway interchange a bit too fast, went off the road and rolled his car several times on the embankment. He was in relatively good spirits, making jokes about what had happened. When I asked him if he was bleeding, he said, "Fuck yeah, bro, I'm bleeding a shitload". After hanging up with him, the very next call was a lady with a toothache. It took me almost five minutes to get the info and start crews because she was screaming bloody murder the whole time. Apparently, her tooth hurt so bad, she couldn't give me her address.

In case you ever get the urge to take a nap on your garage floor, let this be a warning to you: A woman called in one afternoon because her husband had been sleeping in the garage. At some point, a black widow spider crawled into the sleeping man's mouth and bit him in the throat. He was unable to breathe and his throat was swelling. How they knew it was a black widow, I have no idea.

Fresno has *a lot* of neighborhoods that are full of tweakers, miscellaneous transients and drug addicts. In one of our favorite neighborhoods, affectionately referred to as Motel Drive, you can rent rooms by the hour, score your drug of choice and get some chili fries in a one block radius.

There's even a mini-storage facility with working girls occupying most of the units. The drive-thru restaurant, despite their excellent burgers, is a popular spot for hookers and tweakers. I received a call from a young lady outside of this restaurant one afternoon who proceeded to tell me about how a spider bit her arm, laid eggs in the bite hole and now those thousands of baby spiders were hatching and crawling out of her arm. I did, in fact, put the call in for a spider bite and sent the crews. For some reason I doubt they had to spray the rig down with RAID when the call was over. A healthy coat of bleach probably didn't hurt, though.

When I had AJ training with me, we got a call from an individual out in the country, stating the patient was out in a travel-trailer behind the house and was "dead or dying". AJ had been with me for a few weeks and it was time for him to be able to handle the calls (mostly) by himself. He told the caller to go check on the patient and tell us exactly what was going on. Of course, the caller is disabled and not willing or able to do so. Taking a page out of my book, AJ told the caller to hand the phone to someone else. Once we had a second individual on the phone, AJ was able to get him to go out back to the trailer, where he says a third individual is talking to the patient through the trailer door. Now things are starting to sound suspicious. AJ gets the caller to pass the phone off to the third individual and finally finds out that the patient was (only) threatening to kill themselves. This was how a priority one cardiac arrest became a priority three psychiatric problem in under two minutes.

If you ever go to an event or a restaurant that offers discounts to police, fire and military, you'll notice that EMS, being bastard-child of the emergency service sector, is not included. If this is true, then dispatchers are the red-headed, adopted bastard children of public service. Seldom a week goes by that I don't read an article in the newspaper about one of my calls where a "quick-thinking bystander" is credited with saving the life of a patient. A perfect example of this is the time a woman was in line at her neighborhood Grocery Outlet when a man came in and stabbed her in the neck. When I received the call and assessed the situation, I immediately told them to have someone get some towels from within the store and I gave the caller bleeding control instructions. The next day I read the local news and saw the story about how an off-duty correctional officer was credited with saving the woman's life. Get used to it, you're a dispatcher now.

We joke a lot about people who call 911 for ridiculous reasons, such as a stubbed toe or a toothache. The winner of my "Did you really call 911 for that?" award is the lady who called up one day and when I asked her what happened, she said, "I don't know, I think I had a bad dream".

When dealing with scene security, especially with psychiatric patients, we typically ask two questions first: "Are you feeling violent" and "Do you have a weapon there". It always seems odd to me that a caller who is intending on being violent would honestly answer these questions. They usually do, believe it or not. Though, I have to give some honesty credit to the psych patient who answered the second question with "everything's a weapon, bro". He must go to the same dojo as me.

New parents call 911 for anything and everything. Take the woman whose baby had a hair wrapped around her toe, for example. A couple of my favorites (so far) are babies getting stuck in things. One parent called in because they couldn't get their child out of his pool floaties. Again, does nobody own a pair of scissors? The other call was for the fire department to come out to Wendy's to cut a baby out of a high chair. Maybe feed your baby less cheeseburgers?

With a little time, you'll get a feel for cardiac arrests from the first few seconds of a call. Sometimes, though, the caller doesn't know what's going on and you will be on the line as they realize what is actually happening. An old woman had already called us several times over the preceding months for her husband who was prone to falls. She called one day to report that he had fallen in the kitchen while trying to use his walker. To her, this was another typical fall. A minute or so into the call, she realized it wasn't just a regular fall – when I asked her if her husband was breathing. Being elderly and disabled, she was unable to perform any life-saving measures.

Worse, though, was the couple who went to visit their adult son and found him in a chair, tipped over backwards. The mother thought maybe he was passed out. Once I had her go check his breathing, she came to the realization, and told me, that the back of his head was exploded (from the fall or a gunshot or something else, I don't know). She immediately had a meltdown and I couldn't understand another word she said. Luckily for everyone involved (except the patient, maybe), her husband was able to keep it together.

A woman calls in one night, not with the patient, because the patient's mother is freaking out too much to call 911 (but, apparently, could call her sister). All she knew was something was in the thirteen-year old patient's eye. I get the crews started and call the mother to find out what's going on. She tells me about how her son got pinkeye and they gave her some drops at urgent care to give him. Apparently, when it was time to give him the eye drops, she mistakenly grabbed a bottle of fingernail glue and put that in his eye instead of the drops, gluing his eye shut. He RMCT'd.

I was handling one of my first pregnancy/delivery calls. The caller was adamant that she was not going to deliver the baby at home by herself. Unfortunately, she may not have had a choice, so I proceeded with the instructions. One of the first things we tell a caller to do is to get some towels to wrap the baby in, a string or shoelace for the umbilical cord and a safety pin (to pierce the amniotic sac, if needed). When I told her to get the safety pin, her response was, "What?! We ain't doin' no baby killin' up in here today!" Taken aback, I didn't know what to say except, "That's not what it's for, ma'am".

A man calls in to advise that a transformer at a power substation was arcing behind his neighborhood. I get the fire department started right away and begin to question him for further information. As I'm giving him the safety instructions, he lets me know that now the fence behind his neighbor's house was on fire. As with all electrical hazards and fires, I tell the caller to keep everyone away from the hazard. He advises me that one of the neighbors was spraying the fire with a hose. I can hear the caller yelling to them to stop and to move away from the fire. At this point, the engine is turning into the neighborhood and I let the caller off the line so he can wave them down. Two minutes later, the fire department radios in to advise they need EMS code three for an electrocution.

A young lady called 911 in a panic. It took a little work to get her to confirm the address and to tell me what had happened. Turns out her twenty-year old friend had dropped the bong and it broke. Then the friend stepped on it and cut her foot. I wasn't sure if she was so wound up because of the bleeding or because her bong was broken. I managed to calm her down and get her to do bleeding control on the friend's foot. The whole time, she is shouting at her friend to calm down. Pro tip: yelling at someone to calm down does not help them calm down.

For several days in a row, I had received rescue calls for jumpers on freeway overpasses or on multi-story buildings. Each time, they ended up being false. Either there was no patient there, or someone had mistakenly thought someone looking over the edge was a jumper. After about six of these in a week, I was commenting to my colleagues about all the fake jumper calls and whether or not someone ever going to actually do it. The next day, one of my first calls was for a man who jumped off a four-story parking garage.

According to the caller, he was definitely beyond any help – he was splattered all over the street.

A seven-year old called 911 for his little brother having a seizure. Every time I asked him his address, he would just say 222. He was in a massive apartment complex with several different addresses. None of which are 222. I'm sure this is his apartment number. I spend the next couple of minutes trying to figure out where they are by using satellite maps. I ask him if he is by the pool and he says he's by the pool and a pond and the office. This is enough information for me to be able to get the responders to the right location. Now that I know where he is, I can start addressing the patient's medical condition. Just as I begin my questioning, the caller begins screaming that a man was chasing them. I'm trying to figure out who is chasing them and why, as I'm getting the call reconnected with PD. Just before PD picks up, the boy says that the man took his brother and put him into a white van and drove away. PD and I try to ask the caller a few more questions and then the call drops. The boy was calling from a 911-only phone, so we can't call him back. Was it a kidnapping or a helpful adult who wanted to take the boy to the hospital? I never did find out.

Not all medical "professionals" will be as concerned for the care of a patient as you are. In fact, many may be indifferent. I received a call from a nurse at the Oakhurst Health Center, a small-town clinic. She reported there was a lady passed out or having a seizure outside of their clinic in the area by the picnic tables. When I asked her if she was with the patient, she said, "It's not my patient". No, lady, but she is _the_ patient in this circumstance. She refused to answer any questions or provide any aid to the patient, stating, "I'm not going to stay with her, I'm on my lunch."

Sometimes you have to know when a call is too much to handle and ask for help. When Amy was training with me, we received a call for a Gator – basically a souped-up off-road golf cart – that had flipped over into a canal. Come to find out that the Gator was being driven by an eight-year old with three other passengers, around the same age. The call was chaotic, all we could hear were about thirty people all screaming in the background. The caller told us that two of the boys weren't breathing. Amy had been with me about two weeks and had yet to have a real cardiac call. She pointed at me and froze, so I took over the call. Unfortunately, something was going on with my ProQA and the cardiac instructions weren't loading, so I had to give instructions to this frantic caller from memory. She did the best she could relaying the information to the other people on scene and, according to the newspaper, the bystanders were doing CPR. They reported later that night that all of the patients were alive. I found out that both boys died about a week later.

I received a call for an assault at a hotel. We responded out there and the suspect had barricaded himself in the room. The police were notified and they sent out the SWAT team to extract the suspect. An hour or so later, I'm looking at the queue and I see a fire call for the same address. Turns out the suspect decided to set the room on fire instead of coming out. That escalated quickly.

There are some sites that every time you get a call from them, you know something silly is going to happen. We have a few of them. One is a former hotel converted to an addiction treatment facility. Every caller from this location has something off-the-wall to say. Once I got a call from a lady saying she was sunburned and that she burns easily because she is a redhead – and a redhead "down there". The most recent call I took from this facility was for allergies. The patient, knowing she was allergic to bologna (what a strange allergy), decided to eat a bunch of bologna sandwiches and then she couldn't breathe.

When a patient's primary complaint is chest pain or heart problems, one of the questions we will ask is if they took drugs or medications in the past twelve hours. Aside from those people who will list off their twenty prescriptions, the majority of patients will say "no". In a city where *a lot* of people do drugs (*a lot*), I've only had a couple of callers ever admit that they have actually done drugs – less than 0.1%. My favorite, though, was a girl at the phone store who answered that question with, "my uncle made me smoke crack and do heroin and then he stole my stuff".

Hannah's Calls:

The call was for an older lady who lived in the mountains and we were at low levels at the time. It came in as an unconscious call with the RP originally giving cross streets for the location. Being new to dispatch and not realizing all of the other things the RP was saying, I should have realized they were not at the intersection but instead, they were at a residence and wanting to take her mother in the vehicle to the intersection because, in her mind, that would be faster. After putting the call in and identifying the mistake, I quickly told the RP to stay where she was at and to give an accurate address. After establishing a location and asking some preliminary questions, it was evident that the patient was not breathing and needed CPR immediately. The issue was that the RP was hysterical and, being in the mountains, the phone was constantly disconnecting. It felt like every time I would start the instructions, the RP would hang up or the connection would drop. After calling back over and over, I was finally able to keep them on the phone and the RP and her sister were able to follow my directions to perform CPR. It was a grueling 30 minutes of back and forth CPR between the two women. Later, an email was written from the sheriff's office advising that if the dispatcher had not been consistent with CPR instruction the woman would not have lived. I learned two things from this call: 1) Slow down and listen. Just because the person you are talking to is losing their mind does not mean you need to. 2) Regardless of what happens or how you feel about a call, you make a much bigger difference than you think you do as a dispatcher. This call was my third call on my own and it was incredibly overwhelming to experience, but in the end my persistence saved her life.

Another call that had a big impact on my mindset as a dispatcher, again happened with in the first few weeks after I cleared as a dispatcher. PSAP transfers the call over, gives an address and says it is for a shooting but gives no other information. Following that was an ear piercing scream that to this day I still remember. As I tried to navigate the call and figure out what on earth was going on, what I could gather was that the 2 year old in the house found the roommate's gun and shot himself in the head. Probably one of the most difficult calls to handle as a dispatcher. At this point there were three important issues to address in the call; breathing, level of consciousness and serious bleeding. In training they stated in the event of serious bleeding that should be the priority over airway control. I gave control bleeding instructions but the woman was so upset and unsure where the patient was bleeding from that it was almost impossible to give the instructions. Thankfully, law enforcement arrived and, shortly after, EMS and Fire were cleared to roll in. I was pretty bound and determined to not know the outcome of this call, but here is the thing with anything "high profile": it will be all over the media and even though co-workers mean well, they often have a lot of questions and want to talk about everything. It is okay to say you don't want to talk about certain calls and it is okay to talk about them. Finding what works for you is what is important to surviving in this job.

This last call happened a year into dispatching, so it was much easier to navigate through the call and it was much harder to derail me in my pursuit of information. PSAP transfers the call and gives all the information possible to me. Everything from cross streets to clothing description, the works. You know it's about to go down if the law dispatcher stays on the phone and gives every detail of the call before transferring it over and helps by staying on the line to keep the patient focused before disconnecting. This lady was probably one of the funniest individuals I have ever listened to as a dispatcher. She was hysterical! She was not able to focus on any one conversation and continued to talk in circles, but the part that really had me and made me incredibly thankful for the mute button is when the PSAP stated the reason for the call was because she, and I quote, "could not bend properly during intercourse." Now, once you get past being new you stop focusing on all the details of the call and more on what is going on in the big picture and this is when you realize how hilarious people truly are. She proceeds to tell me about how she and her boyfriend laid the blanket out so they can have sex. When I asked her what her name was she stopped talking and told me, "I don't know." I was perplexed and laughing all at the same time. This lady really could not keep her story straight. She would randomly go on a tangent not at all related to what we were talking about. In the end, she hung up on me but I was pretty thankful since I could not stop laughing at this point.

Alicia's Call:
      There will always be a few calls that will sit with you forever. As much as you try to shake it off, they still make an impact. One in particular, for me, started off as nothing unusual: a parent calling in to have their child taken to a pysch facility again. This patient had just been released from a program earlier that week and was having a hard time adjusting at home. The mom was going through all of the scene security questions and all of the pysch questions calmly, all the while talking to her son in between answering my questions. I could hear the concern and compassion in her voice and maybe a little fear for the well-being of her child. You have to understand what sets this apart from other pysch calls; for the most part, we get parents who call

because, at some level, they have tapped out, they really have no more energy to give to their child. This call was different because the mom was telling her child how much she loves him and asking him what shoes he was going to wear, since he couldn't have shoe laces. As a mom, you hope that you never have to watch your child suffer or go through any type of pain. I was touched so much by the words that she was saying that I had tears running down my cheeks. I placed her on mute to try to compose myself. At that point I hear her tell him she loves him unconditionally and everything will be okay. I just couldn't click back on. At that point I wasn't able to separate myself from the caller. I had my partner take over the call while I took a few minutes to collect myself.

GLOSSARY OF TERMS

Apparatus – A piece of fire equipment, such as an engine, truck or brush rig.
Bariatric – Having to do with obese or overweight patients.
CAD – Computer Aided Dispatch. The interface used to input call information and to assign responders.
Calling Party – The individual calling in for service (see RP). A first-party caller is the patient, victim or anybody calling for themselves. A second-party caller is someone with the patient or immediately involved with the incident. A third-party caller is a passerby or uninvolved witness.
COPD – Chronic Obstructive Pulmonary Disease. One or more of several lung disorders, such as chronic bronchitis or emphysema.
Detrimental Reliance – A legal time defining promises made by emergency services and their ability to deliver on the promise. Failure to deliver could create liability for the dispatcher or responder, as the caller could seek other means of help.
ED-Q – Emergency Dispatcher Quality Assurance. An individual who reviews emergency calls and provides feedback for improvement.
EFD – Emergency Fire Dispatcher.
EMD – Emergency Medical Dispatcher.
EPD – Emergency Police Dispatcher.
Hazmat – Hazardous Materials. Any chemical, liquid, gas or solid, which poses a threat to life, health or property.

IAED – International Academy of Emergency Dispatch. An organization that develops and reviews emergency dispatch protocols and procedures.

LVN, MD, NP, PA, RN – Levels of medical certification who are typically equipped to provide care on their own, without dispatch instruction or intervention (BLS certified). They stand for Licensed Vocational Nurse, Medical Doctor, Nurse Practitioner, Physician's Assistant and Registered Nurse. Please note, MA and CNA are not on this list.

Positive Ambiguity – Providing reassurance to a caller without making any promises. For example, saying "We will be there as fast as we can" as opposed to "We will be there in five minutes".

Preceptor – An experienced dispatcher responsible for training new employees.

Priority – The level of response. Typically, priority one is lights and sirens with maximum resources while priority three is without lights and sirens with minimum appropriate resources. These are typically the opposite of codes – where Code 3 is highest priority.

Problem Nature – The general reason for response with minimum detail. For example – Falls, Fire, Robbery, et al.

PSAP – Public Safety Answering Point. Any facility that receives emergency calls. Typically the primary PSAP is law enforcement, secondary is fire and tertiary is EMS. Many call centers function as more than one level of PSAP.

RMCT – Refused Medical Care and Treatment. A patient who declines ambulance or first responder services.
RP – Reporting Party. The individual making the call to 911. Sometimes used to mean Responsible Party. For instance, in the case of a fire alarm, the RP may be the individual who is being sent to unlock the building, even if they are not the reporting party.
Unit – Any piece of EMS or law enforcement responder equipment. Such as an ambulance or patrol car.
UTL – Unable to Locate. When a responder is unable to find a patient, victim or suspect.
VIN – Vehicle Identification Number. A number unique to each vehicle which is not removable or interchangeable. Different from a license plate.

QUIZ YOURSELF

Here are a few scenarios you can read through and think about how you would handle the situation. My solutions or answers are at the end of the section.

Scenario One: A caller reports a heavy amount of smoke coming from the back yard of a house. They are driving by and are unable to tell you what is on fire.

Do you select the problem nature Structure Fire, Outside Fire or Smoke Investigation?

Scenario Two: First-party caller reports they are depressed and want to harm themselves. Which problem nature do you choose?

While you are on the call, the patient reports that they took a bottle of pills. What do you do?

Scenario Three: Caller reports that their child was running in the house, thought the sliding glass door was open and ran into it. The door broke, causing the patient to fall and also cut them and they are now bleeding. Is the most appropriate problem nature Falls, Hemorrhage or Traumatic Injury?

Scenario Four: Caller advises they smell something strange inside their house. They are unsure where the odor is coming from and say it smells like rotten eggs. What could this be?

Scenario Five: You have a first-party caller who is hard to understand because they are slurring their speech. They are reporting that they can't move their left arm. What is the most appropriate problem nature?

Scenario Six: Second-party caller reports that their diabetic grandfather is kind of out of it and is acting strange. What could be going on with him?

Scenario Seven: Patient calls to report that they have COPD, diabetes and congestive heart failure. For the last few days, they have been feeling sick and are reporting a fever of 101. They are completely alert and don't have any difficulty speaking between breaths. What is the most relevant problem nature?

Scenario Eight: A first-party caller reports that the roof of their house is on fire. You are having difficulty getting any additional information because they are panicked and screaming for you to "hurry up". What is the most important thing to address?

Scenario Nine: A second-party caller reports that they just saw someone get stabbed in front of the liquor store. They hang up before you can collect any additional information. What do you do?

Scenario Ten: An eight-year old caller reports that their mom is having a seizure. They are at home, but don't know their address. What are some things you can do to try to get their location?

Answers:
1) Because you don't know what, if anything, is on fire, the most appropriate response would be Smoke Investigation. This will typically get fewer apparatus assigned than an outside or a structure fire. It's important that we not dispatch unnecessary resources when possible. The first arriving apparatus will call for additional crews if there is a working fire.
2) If someone is threatening suicide, it should be addressed as a psychiatric emergency. If they are actively committing and act of self-harm, it should be addressed as the method which they are harming themselves – in this case, overdose/poisoning. The first thing you should do is address scene security, holding back EMS responders and dispatching law

enforcement as necessary. Once determining what the patient has taken, you can conference in poison control for advice on what can be done until help arrives.

3) Generally, we want to choose the mechanism of injury over the symptoms or result of the mechanism. In this case, a traumatic injury (running into the door) caused the fall and the bleeding, so traumatic injury would be the most appropriate problem nature.

4) This is a potential natural gas leak. Natural gas is often scented to make it easily identifiable. Likewise, propane is often scented like garlic or onions for the same reason. If a caller reports a smell like chemicals, it could be a Hazmat situation and caution should be used when sending crews.

5) The common indicators for a stroke are slurred speech, numbness or paralysis on one side, facial droop, sudden and severe headache, vision problems and loss of balance or coordination. This patient has two of these symptoms, so I would put it in for a stroke.

6) A diabetic who is not alert, behaving abnormally or is combative may be having a blood-sugar crisis. I would send a crew out for a diabetic problem.

7) I would send the crews out for the fever. While the chronic conditions can have

serious complications, the patient is not reporting difficulty breathing, blood sugar abnormality or heart problems and they aren't presenting symptoms over the phone, we should go with their reported complaint, which is fever.
8) The first thing to address would be getting everybody out of the house and to a safe location. This happened when I was training an intern and she did not realize that the caller was panicking because they were in a burning house. She continued to try to ask questions irrelevant to the patient's safety and I had to take over and tell her to get the caller out of the house before asking any additional questions.
9) Because we don't have any additional information about this call, I would err on the side of caution and hold the crews back and get law enforcement started to secure the scene. Then we can call the RP back and try to gather additional information about the scene and the patient's condition.
10) There are several options here (see Section II). First, put the call in for wherever their phone is pinging to get the crews going in the right direction. If they are in an apartment, I'd ask if they know the name of their apartment. If not, I'd first ask them to find a piece of mail. You can also ask them to find their mom's purse and get her driver's license and read you the address on there

(hopefully it's correct). They may not know their address, but they might know what street they live on and which street they turn on to get there. You can ask them what school they go to and how far the school is from their house (do they walk to school?). Do they have the number of their other parent, grandparent, older sibling or aunt/uncle? You can have another dispatcher start calling those numbers for an address or directions. If your GPS is relatively close, you can get on street view and ask them questions about their neighborhood like what color is your house, do you have a fence, is there a tree in your front yard, etc. I often hesitate to ask a child to go out of the house to get help, but if none of the other options work, I may ask them to go to the neighbor's house to ask the address.

TEN THINGS EVERY DISPATCHER WANTS YOU TO KNOW

1) **Stay calm.** If we can't understand what you're saying, we can't get help to you.

2) **Answer our questions.** When we have all of the information we need, we can send you the best quality help.

3) **Don't be an asshole.** Yelling, screaming and calling names will not get you help any faster. In fact, it delays our ability to get valuable information that our crews will need when they arrive.

4) **Stay on the line.** Hanging up on a 911 dispatcher is just going to delay us getting responders to you by however long it takes us to call you back and get you to answer. We will keep calling.

5) **Know where you are.** Give us an address, the cross streets or the name of the business where you are located. GPS isn't always accurate. If we can't find you, we can't help you.

6) **Keep it simple.** We don't need to know your whole life history, just tell us what's going on right now.

7) **Follow instructions.** What we are telling you to do isn't because we like to hear ourselves talk - it could be a matter of saving a life before the responders arrive.

8) **Only call in an emergency.** The 911 system is bogged down by non-emergency calls and unless you're calling for a true emergency, you're taking away our time from someone who may truly need it. Every police, fire and EMS agency has a non-emergency number. Please use them.

9) **Stop saying "hurry up".** We are not the one's coming to your emergency. Our whole industry is based on hurrying up and we always send help as fast as we can. The best thing you can do to get service faster is to just answer our questions and save any extra comments.

10) **For the love of god, stay calm.** Seriously, save your melt down for later.

Our goal is to get responders on their way to you in under thirty seconds. We can only do this with your cooperation.

A martial artist knelt before his master sensei in a ceremony to receive the hard-earned Black Belt. After years of relentless training, the student has finally reached a pinnacle of achievement in the discipline.

"Before granting you the belt, you must pass one more test," the sensei solemnly tells the young man.

"I'm ready," responds the student, expecting perhaps one more round of sparring.

"You must answer the essential question, 'What is the true meaning of the Black Belt?'"

"Why, the end of my journey," says the student. "A well-deserved reward for all of my hard work."

The master waits for more. Clearly, he is not satisfied. The sensei finally speaks: "You are not ready for the Black Belt. Return in one year."

As the student kneels before his master a year later, he is again asked the question, "What is the true meaning of the Black Belt?"

"A symbol of distinction and the highest achievement in our art," the young man responds.

Again the master waits for more. Still unsatisfied, he says once more: "You are not ready for the Black Belt. Return in one year."

A year later the student kneels before his sensei and hears the question, "What is the true meaning of the Black Belt?"

This time he answers, "The Black Belt represents not the end, but the beginning, the start of a never-ending journey of discipline, work and the pursuit of an ever-higher standard."

"Yes," says the master. *"You are now ready to receive the Black Belt and begin your work."*

Made in United States
Orlando, FL
05 December 2022